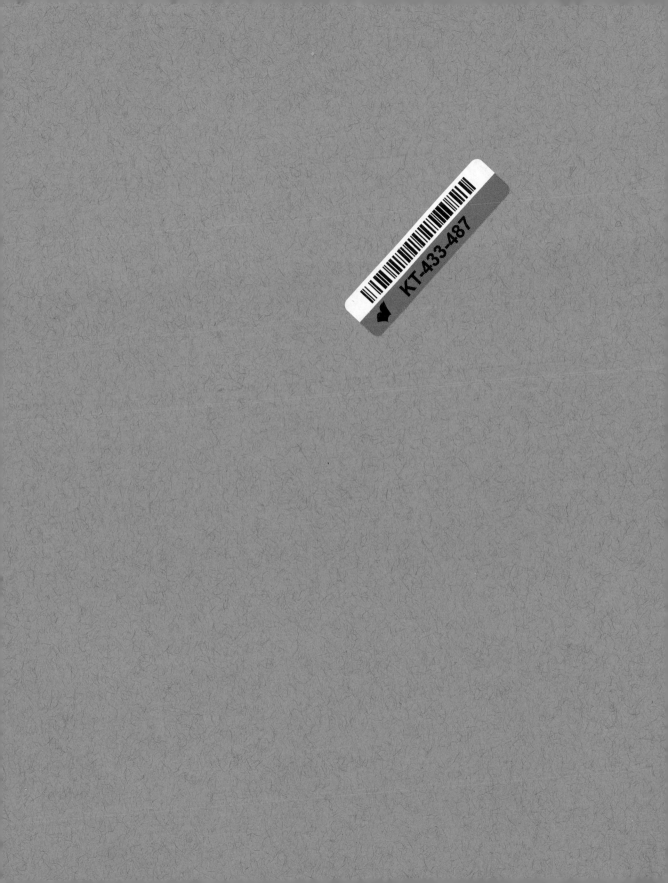

WHAT WE SAW | *CBS News, with an Introduction by Dan Rather*

SIMON & SCHUSTER

NEW YORK   LONDON   TORONTO   SYDNEY   SINGAPORE

SIMON & SCHUSTER
Rockefeller Center
1230 Avenue of the Americas
New York, NY 10020

SIMON & SCHUSTER and colophon are registered trademarks of
Simon & Schuster, Inc.

Permissions acknowledgments appear on page 142.

For information about special discounts for bulk purchases,
please contact Simon & Schuster Special Sales:
1-800-456-6798 or business@simonandschuster.com

Edited by Susan Ellingwood
Design by VERTIGO DESIGN, NYC

Manufactured in the United States of America

10 9 8 7 6 5 4 3 2 1

Library of Congress Cataloging-in-Publication Data

What we saw / CBS News ; with an introduction by Dan Rather.
p. cm.
1. September 11 Terrorist Attacks, 2001—Personal narratives. 2. September 11
Terrorist Attacks, 2001—Press coverage.   I. CBS News.
HV6432.W46 2002
973.931—dc21   2002075811
ISBN 0-7432-4190-8

CONTENTS

IT HAS BECOME ALMOST A MATTER OF CONVENTION TO TALK ABOUT
September 11, 2001, in terms of where one was when one first heard
the news. I think it is part of an understandable quest to discover
that precise point in time, that bridging nanosecond, between life
before and life after. We are trying to recall the feel of things as we
knew them and to discover just what changed—and how—in that
instant when we became aware that this day would be different from
all the days that had preceded it. For the record, then, I had just
stepped out of the shower when I heard a bulletin come over the
radio: Smoke was coming from the World Trade Center, and there
were reports that a plane had hit one of the towers.

For me, though—and I suspect this is also true for others—the
true force of September 11 was revealed not in a single moment but
in a series of moments. In the wake of the first tower's collapse, a
correspondent phoned in after having been nearly overcome by
the choking cloud of smoke and dust. After the second tower fell,
another reporter, a woman new to the city, told of having her life
saved by a member of the New York City Fire Department. With
debris raining down and roiling in all directions, this firefighter
pressed her against a wall. She could feel his heart beating against her
back. She had been sure, she said, that this was how she would die.
And later in the day, there were the pictures of doctors assembled
outside St. Vincent's Medical Center, waiting to perform triage on
thousands of wounded who never arrived.

These moments marched alongside the indelible images of that day, each further advancing an understanding of the attacks' toll. Each giving added confirmation to New York City mayor Rudolph W. Giuliani's statement that we were looking at a "tremendous" loss of life—"More," as he put it, "than we can bear."

Long ago, when America was still young, Nathaniel Hawthorne wrote: "Time flies over us, but leaves its shadows behind." For now and for the foreseeable future, we stand in the shadows of that terrible, clear morning. We live in a world remade by the attacks of September 11. Years will pass, and the photos and videos will age and fade. Our memories of the feelings attached to them in real time will also dim, as they have already. But echoes will continue to reverberate from that date.

For more than forty years, reporting for CBS News has given me a front-row seat on history. When big events occur, they always loom large in the present. And there are times when the television screen enlarges what the perspective of years will show to be stories of only passing importance. The inherent drama of the special report—the break-in during regular programming—and the modern broadcasting phenomenon of "blanket coverage" have a way of giving apparent equal weight to the many different calamities that set them in motion. For example, if one were to judge solely on the basis of television news hours, one might come away with the impression that the death of John F. Kennedy, Jr., was as important a news story as the assassination of John F. Kennedy, Sr. It isn't a question of ranking tragedies but of gauging the historical impact—the far-ranging repercussions —of a story. And it is rare, in the fury of the moment, that these historical implications are reckoned with accuracy.

September 11 was one of those rare times. When the event happened, while it happened, we knew we were watching history unfold. We saw a line—a shadow—fall over the newsreel of our lives, one that would forever mark the days after as separate from the days before. We understood that we would remember, would someday tell our grandchildren, where we had been and what we had been doing when we heard the news. The TV screen did not enlarge that day, not when New Yorkers could see the twin towers burning with their own eyes, not when people in our nation's capital could see a cloud of smoke billowing from the Pentagon. If anything, television reduced the horrible images to a size that could be comprehended.

Of course, the historical impact of any event depends on the reactions that follow in its wake. The attacks of September 11 have provoked not only a direct response—or series of responses—but also a larger and more profound change in how our nation interacts with the rest of our world. From the Middle East to South America, from the Persian Gulf to Central Asia and the Pacific Rim, the war on terrorism now provides the impetus and the context for American foreign policy. Indeed, an atmosphere of change prevails all around the world. Alliances are shifting. In the danger zones of the globe, there is a sense that once static situations are again "in play." Some historians have compared the current state of affairs to that just before the outbreak of World War I, when great powers sought political advantage in Europe. Others invoke the years that immediately followed World War II, the period of rising tensions that gave birth to the cold war. Whatever the point of comparison, the message is clear: As with those eras, our time is witness to a tectonic shift in international relations.

Such are the aftershocks that have continued and will continue to follow the earthquake that was September 11. This book and DVD represent an effort by CBS News to chronicle the early hours, days, and weeks of this seismic jolt. They are intended as historical documents and reminders—reminders not only of the fact that terror struck on a beautiful fall day but of the pictures, sounds, and emotions that accompanied the attacks and our first efforts to deal with them, as a nation united in fear, anger, grief, and determination.

Much has been written and said about the effect of September 11 on America: that it awakened us from our illusions of invulnerability, that it shattered the sense of insularity that complacency and prosperity had let creep into our national discourse. These observations sting, but there is truth in them. And like so many Americans of all professions, September 11 forced those of us who report the news to reevaluate what we do and how we do it.

For me and my colleagues at CBS News, the scale of this story—and the many stories that have flowed from it—has given us an opportunity to do the kind of journalism to which we aspire. It is a chance to perform a public service, to report news that is not only gripping but that also matters. From what I've seen in the year between then and now, it is a chance that has been seized upon by much if not most of America's working press. The focus, for now, is on the truly important. International coverage is up. It is not yet at the levels where it should be, and it may prove to be a temporary development, but for the moment the news reflects and informs America's renewed outward gaze.

However painfully, we have received an education. But it has not only been an education of the mind. Our hearts have learned much, too. We have been confronted by the courage of the firefighters and police who answered the call at the World Trade Center and the Pentagon, by the ordinary citizens who gave their lives to deter United Airlines Flight 93 from its murderous path, by the fighting men and women who travel far and give so much to defend our country. The exhaustive labors of emergency workers and volunteers at Ground Zero have taught us new lessons in loyalty and love. Each flag-draped stretcher and coffin, every moment of silence, has given us a new appreciation of the word *respect*. The dry rattle of a funeral drum, the plaintive wail of bagpipes playing "Amazing Grace"—these sounds summon our deepest feelings with a new sincerity, to a degree that may have made us blush in the past.

But the past, as it has been said, is a foreign land. It is in the spirit of understanding the distance we have come in a year that CBS News offers this collection of remembrances from the day—and the days that followed—when we were first pulled, blinking and confused and very much against our wills, across the border to the lives we know now.

Dan Rather
CBS News
New York City

CHRONOLOGY OF EVENTS | *September 11, 2001 (EDT)*

8:00 A.M. ›

American Airlines Flight 11 leaves Logan International Airport in Boston bound for Los Angeles with 81 passengers and 11 crew members on board.

8:14 A.M. ›

United Airlines Flight 175 leaves Logan International Airport bound for Los Angeles with 56 passengers and nine crew members on board.

8:21 A.M. ›

American Flight 77 leaves Washington Dulles International Airport bound for Los Angeles with 58 passengers and six crew members on board.

8:42 A.M. ›

United Flight 93 leaves Newark International Airport in New Jersey bound for San Francisco with 38 passengers and seven crew members on board.

8:48 A.M. ›

American Flight 11 crashes into Tower 1 (the North Tower) of the World Trade Center complex in New York City, killing everyone on board.

9:41 A.M. ›

American Flight 77 crashes into the Pentagon, outside Washington, D.C., killing everyone on the plane and more than 100 Defense Department employees.

9:50 A.M. ›

The South Tower of the World Trade Center collapses.

10:03 A.M. ›

United Flight 93 crashes in a field outside Shanksville, Pennsylvania, killing everyone on board.

10:29 A.M. ›

The North Tower of the World Trade Center collapses. More than 2,500 workers and hundreds of firefighters are killed in the collapse of the Twin Towers.

10:30 A.M. ›

New York State governor George E. Pataki declares a state of emergency in New York, primary elections are postponed, and Mayor Rudolph W. Giuliani orders lower Manhattan evacuated.

9:03 A.M. ›
United Flight 175 crashes into Tower 2 (the South Tower) of the World Trade Center, killing everyone on board.

9:08 A.M. ›
The Federal Aviation Administration closes all New York–area airports and the airspace over the city.

9:21 A.M. ›
The Port Authority of New York and New Jersey closes all bridges and tunnels in the metropolitan area.

9:26 A.M. ›
The FAA grounds all nonmilitary planes and cancels all flights into and out of the United States.

9:30 A.M. ›
President George W. Bush delivers his first official remarks from Sarasota, Florida.

12:36 P.M. ›
President Bush speaks to the nation in a televised statement from Barksdale Air Force Base in Louisiana.

1:27 P.M. ›
A state of emergency is declared in Washington, D.C.

2:30 P.M. ›
The FAA announces that there will be no commercial air traffic into or out of the United States for at least 24 hours.

6:10 P.M. ›
Mayor Giuliani encourages all New Yorkers to take the day (Wednesday, September 12) off.

8:30 P.M.
President Bush speaks to the nation on television from the Oval Office.

IT'S 8:52 HERE IN NEW YORK, I'M BRYANT GUMBEL. We understand that there has been a plane crash on the southern tip of Manhattan. . . .We understand that a plane has crashed into the World Trade Center.

We don't know anything more than that. We don't know if it was a commercial aircraft. We don't know if it was a private aircraft. We have no idea how many were on board or what the extent of the injuries are.

Right now, we have, I understand, an eyewitness on the phone. Sir, good morning, this is Bryant Gumbel. Could you give us your name?

> STEWART NURICK: My name is Stewart.
>
> GUMBEL: Stewart, where are you right now?
>
> NURICK: I'm working at a restaurant in SoHo.
>
> GUMBEL: All right, so tell us what you saw if you would.
>
> NURICK: I was waiting a table, and I literally saw a . . . it seemed to be a small plane . . . I just heard a couple noises, it looked like it bounced off the building, and then I just saw a huge ball of fire on top of the building. And just lots of smoke and what looked to be debris or glass falling down. It happened really quickly.
>
> GUMBEL: Can you tell us about the scene down there right now?
>
> NURICK: Right now people are just on the street looking at the building. It's not too crazy down where I am.
>
> GUMBEL: Okay, Stewart, I thank you very much.

We're on the line with another eyewitness. Sir, this is Bryant Gumbel in New York. Wendell Clyne, tell me where you are if you would.

WENDELL CLYNE: Well, right now I'm in the hotel offices here.

GUMBEL: Where were you when the . . .

CLYNE: I was standing right in front of the hotel. I'm the doorman.

GUMBEL: Which hotel?

CLYNE: The Marriott World Trade Center.

GUMBEL: Okay, so you were standing outside. Tell us what you saw and what you heard.

CLYNE: I heard first an explosion. And I just figured that it was a plane passing by. Then all of sudden, stuff just started falling like bricks and paper and everything. And so I just kind of ran inside to get away from the falling debris and glass. Then when it kind of stopped, I heard a guy screaming. Where I looked over, there was a guy that was on fire, so I ran over and I tried to put the fire out on him. And he was screaming. I just told him to roll, roll, and he said he couldn't. And then another guy came over . . . and put the flames out on him.

GUMBEL: All right, Mr. Clyne, thank you very much, sir.

I understand Theresa Renaud is with us right now. Ms. Renaud, good morning. This is Bryant Gumbel, I'm down on 59th and 5th. Where are you?

THERESA RENAUD: I am in Chelsea, and we are at 8th and 16th. We're in the tallest building in the area, and my window faces south, so it looks directly onto the World Trade Center. Approximately ten minutes ago there was a major explosion from about the 80th floor—looks like it's affected probably four to eight floors. Major flames are coming out of the north side and also the east side of the building. It was a very loud explosion, followed by flames, and it looks like the building is still on fire on the inside.

Oh, there's another one—another plane just hit. [gasps; yelling] Oh, my God! Another plane has just hit—it hit another building, flew right into the middle of it. My God, it's right in the middle of the building.

GUMBEL: This one into [Tower 2]?

RENAUD: Yes, yes, right in the middle of the building. . . . That was definitely . . . on purpose.

GUMBEL: Why do you say that was definitely on purpose?

RENAUD: Because it just flew straight into it.

"The Numbers" [EXCERPT]

by Bryan Charles, in BEFORE AND AFTER STORIES FROM NEW YORK

EDITED BY Thomas Beller, PUBLISHED BY Mr. Beller's Neighborhood Books

I walked over to the window from my cubicle in 2 World Trade Center. All I saw were thousands of papers flying through the air. Some of the papers were burning. . . .

Without realizing what I was doing, I went back to my desk, got my backpack, and walked to the hallway near the elevators, where people had already congregated . . . I don't remember any one person suggesting that we get in the stairwell. I know I didn't say it. Probably it was a collective decision. All I know is that the door opened and we filed in. It was packed, two lanes, shoulder to shoulder with workers from the higher floors already making their way down. I looked at the sign by the door that said 70 and took my first step . . .

A few floors later, maybe ten, maybe less, came another explosion. This one was loud. . . . The tower shook. I slipped down the stairs. People screamed and gripped the railing to keep from falling. The building,

this enormous skyscraper, this national landmark, swayed back and forth. . . . This is it, I thought. Get ready to go down with the ship. My body and mind went numb. I didn't start praying, I didn't have visions of childhood, I didn't see my life flash before my eyes. I went into this white arctic zone of either acceptance or resignation or preparedness. I don't know what it was. I was blank. I was nothing. People screamed, they prayed. The screams and prayers merged into one. . . .

Sometimes the line in the stairwell stopped cold. Congestion on the lower floors. We'd be standing in the stairwell, not moving forward, with voices above screaming, "No! Don't stop! Go down! Keep moving! . . ." Every few minutes I called out the words "It's gonna be okay." I didn't believe myself but kept saying it anyway. One time when the line was stalled, I turned to the guy behind me. We smiled weakly at each other and shook hands. . . .

After the explosion, life became a matter of watching the numbers on the signs in the stairwell get smaller. It was a long, slow process. Forty. Thirty-nine. Thirty-eight. Thirty-seven. Thirty-six. . . . I couldn't tell how long we'd been in there. Time had vanished. There was no time. There was only descent. There was only counting and waiting and counting, circling around again and again. . . . Then we wound down the last ten floors. We came out on the plaza level. . . . It was then that I realized something had happened that was far more terrifying than any of us had thought being blind and dumb in the stairwell. ▮

IN MAY 2001, MY BROTHER, GEDEON, and I, along with our friend James Hanlon, a New York City fireman, began filming a documentary at FDNY's Engine 7, Ladder 1. The purpose of the film was to chronicle the nine-month probationary period of twenty-one-year-old Tony Benetatos, a recent graduate of the Fire Academy who had been assigned to this firehouse in lower Manhattan.

We spent the summer following Tony and capturing life at the firehouse. But as fall approached, we realized that we were missing a crucial element to a documentary about firefighters: a fire. You see, Tony never seemed to be on duty when his company was called to a fire.

That changed on Tuesday, September 11, 2001. The day started out as any other at the firehouse. Guys started coming in around 8:00 A.M. to relieve those who had been working the night before. At 8:30 A.M., a call came in about a possible gas leak at the corner of Lispenard and Church streets, a few blocks away from the firehouse. I rode in the battalion car, as I usually did, filming the chief.

As the units were gathering around the suspected gas leak, we heard a roaring sound that got closer and louder. I remember looking up and seeing an American Airlines jet pass between two buildings. I immediately pointed the camera to where the plane was headed. Two seconds later the jet crashed into Tower 1, the north tower of the World Trade Center.

The firefighters rushed to their trucks and departed for the Trade Center, which was about fifteen blocks away. I jumped into the battalion car and continued filming as Chief Joseph Pfeifer gave the initial report of the collision. We arrived at Tower 1 in less than three minutes.

From the very beginning the devastation was apparent. Smoke was pouring out of the tower, and evidently jet fuel had run down the elevator shaft, creating a fireball in the lobby. People were severely burned and all the windows had been blown out. As the minutes passed, hundreds of firefighters from across the city reported to the command post, which was set up in the lobby, and were sent up to evacuate people in the tower. There was a mood of confidence in the lobby. I can recall looking at firefighters and seeing a determination and eagerness to do their job. In my mind, there was never any doubt that they would quell the fire, and being with members of the best fire department in the world, I wasn't afraid.

Suddenly we heard an explosion coming from outside, and as I turned to look out the windows, I saw flaming debris falling in the courtyard and then heard a radio call announcing that Tower 2 had been hit by another plane. Any thought that this was simply a terrible accident vanished: New York was under attack.

That is when the horrible crashing sounds started and never stopped. People trapped on the upper floors, cornered by fire and smoke, jumped from the tower and landed outside the lobby in a loud crash. At first I thought that the bodies were pieces of the building, but then a firefighter next to me said, "We got jumpers." Every thirty seconds that

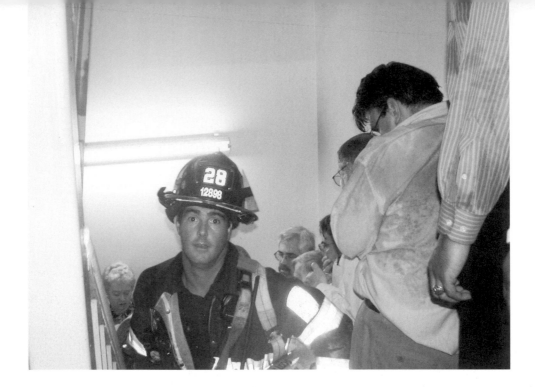

same crashing sound would resonate throughout the lobby. It is probably the thing that will stay with me always, the realization that every time I heard this sound, it was a life that was gone.

At about 10:00 A.M., as I was filming the chiefs in the lobby coordinating the rescue, we heard a loud crushing noise coming from above us. Everyone started to run. We thought the tower was coming down on us. After running fifty feet into an adjacent room, I fell to the floor, waiting and hoping for a quick and painless death. A few seconds passed and the noise faded, replaced by a cloud of dust. Although we didn't realize it at the time, Tower 2 had collapsed.

I turned on the light on top of my camera and went back to filming. But something was different. Before I was filming because I wanted to document what was happening. Now I was filming to put distance between myself and the horrible scene that I was witnessing through my camera lens.

I remember filming Chief Pfeifer as he gave the evacuation order to all units in Tower 1. For him, it was a precaution: We didn't know what had happened to Tower 2, and Pfeifer just wanted everyone out to re-group and assess the situation. As we were trying to get out of the tower, we came across the body of the Fire Department chaplain, Father Mychal Judge, who had been killed by falling debris. Four firefighters carried him out of the building. It took us about twenty minutes to find a safe way to exit.

Since we didn't know that Tower 2 had collapsed, we never thought the same could happen to Tower 1. But at 10:28 A.M., at the corner of West and Vesey streets, just 400 feet away, the north tower started to come down. We ran for our lives. I lay down in the street and felt someone jump on top of me as the cloud of dust and debris enveloped me for the second time. After a few minutes, the person on top of me got up and told me to follow him. It was the voice of Chief Pfeifer.

DAN RATHER | *Correspondent, CBS News:*

THIS IS CBS NEWS CONTINUING LIVE COVERAGE of the apparent terrorist attacks today here in New York City, and in Washington, D.C. It's important to say that there is much that is not known. There have been some terrible things happening, but until and unless we know the facts, it's very difficult to draw many conclusions.

Now, here's what we know. Just before 9 Eastern Time, this morning, a plane crashed into one of the Twin Towers of the World Trade Center along the Hudson River here in New York. A few minutes later, a second plane crashed into the other tower. Both skyscrapers are on fire; evacuations have been under way for a long while. There are known injuries. How many? Much too soon to know. And whether there's any death or not, it is too soon to know. Yes, there are widespread assumptions that there must be death, but there are no confirmed fatalities.

Now in Washington, the Pentagon has had a fire. There is much speculation of what would have caused the fire and explosion at the Pentagon.
One eyewitness, and only one so far, is quoted as saying he thinks—I
put that in quotation marks—he thinks a plane crashed into the Pentagon. But there will be rumors all day and we're going to try to separate
the rumors from the facts.

We go to Jim Stewart in our Washington Bureau. Jim?

JIM STEWART | *Correspondent, CBS News:*

DAN, HERE IN WASHINGTON, the police now have closed down the Capitol, the House, and the Senate. They have closed down the Justice Department, the World Bank has been emptied. We are told that the Metropolitan Police Department of Washington is on full alert with the anticipation that there could be additional targets if in fact someone is targeting sites in the nation's capital. We are told that the FAA has grounded all domestic flights in the United States.

One building that has not closed down is the FBI. The FBI has established an emergency command post in the center of its building. It's a contained area that is presumably safe from bombs. FBI officials have been there for the last two hours, trying to sort out exactly what is going on. I can tell you, Dan, that the working theory here is that this is the work of terrorists. They specifically believe this is the work of Osama bin Laden. But this is pure speculation at the moment.

PETER MAER | *CBS Radio News Correspondent:*

I'M PETER MAER OUTSIDE THE WHITE HOUSE, which is now being evacuated. Secret Service officers, some here looking very concerned, are ordering everybody out of the building. Staffers and reporters are streaming out. We're quickly moving toward the Pennsylvania Avenue exit. In the distance, in the narrow open space between the White House and the neighboring Executive Office Building, black smoke, thick smoke, can be seen in the sky coming from the direction of the Pentagon, which according to word from some here has been hit by a plane. All of this as a very uncertain situation develops at the World Trade Center in New York.

Fire trucks and other emergency vehicles are racing through the streets, but there is no immediate evidence of any fire or accident. There is no sign of any problem here near the White House itself.

Outside the gates now, almost all eyes are looking skyward. Police are training binoculars upward, apparently watching for more aircraft. People are just streaming out of nearby office buildings—it is very much a scene verging on chaos. The streets are near gridlock, and very worried-looking people are rushing out of government offices and other buildings.

HAROLD DOW | *Correspondent, CBS News:*

AS I MADE MY WAY TO THE WORLD TRADE CENTER on that Tuesday morning after the jetliners had crashed into both towers, I could hear sirens coming from all over the city—police cars, ambulances, fire engines. But it was what I saw that disturbed me the most: bodies falling from the sky. At first I didn't know what they were. But as they came closer into view, I could see that they were men and women, their shirts and hair blowing in the wind. A woman standing near me cried out, "Oh, no." Others just stared in disbelief. As I stood there stunned and numb, I thought about the twenty-nine years I've been working for CBS News and how I'm supposed to be ready for anything. As another body fell, I knew instantly, "No way am I ready for this."

About two blocks from the towers, at the corner of Barclay and Washington streets, police officers were trying to evacuate people from the area. They didn't care if you had a press pass. But then I spotted an undercover police officer I had done a story on a few years back. I asked if he could get me closer. He was a little apprehensive and kept mumbling, "This thing could go, this thing could go." In the back of my mind I thought, "There's no way this building is coming down." He was reluctant but he did help me get closer.

As we moved in I noticed that the emergency vehicles had surrounded the buildings and officials had set up command posts. Firemen, police officers, and other emergency workers were rushing into the towers.

I was about a block away. That's when I heard what sounded like a freight train: the noise twisted steel makes when it's under a lot of stress. Then there was the rumbling sound of the floors collapsing on top of each other, each floor with its own gush of air. I looked up and saw Tower Number Two crumbling down. Debris was falling everywhere. My eyes locked onto my friend the undercover cop. He was scared and so was I. He ran in one direction and I ran in another. I looked back. A

huge ball of black smoke and concrete dust at the base of Tower Two was heading in my direction.

Hundreds of people started running. Some fell, either tripped or were hit with falling debris. You couldn't stop running because if you did you would be trampled. I turned a few corners and ran down a street that was littered with shoes. People had literally run out of their shoes, fleeing for their lives.

The smoke was choking; it was hard to see. That's when I spotted the Chambers Street subway stop. I knew it would be my only way out of this chaos, so I took it. About three people followed me. I ran down the stairs, looked over to the right, and noticed a shoe repair shop. All four of us ran inside and shut the door behind us. Within seconds that dense cloud of smoke made its way down into the subway, but we were safe.

The owner of the shoe repair shop, who was wearing a turban and had olive-colored skin and a beard, allowed me to use his phone and within seconds I was live on the air with Dan Rather. He wanted to know if I could confirm that one of the towers had come down. It was hard to believe what I had just witnessed and it pained me to say it: "Yes, Dan, I can confirm that one of the towers is down."

"Death Takes Hold Among the Living"

by Pete Hamill, DAILY NEWS, September 12, 2001

We were gathered at a large table in the Tweed Courthouse, discussing over bagels and coffee its future as a symbol of civilization, a museum of the history of New York. About 8:45, we heard a boom. It was not a ferocious boom, but the sort too common in a city where construction jobs are a constant. A few made nervous jokes and the meeting went on. We heard sirens now. Then, just before 9, a man came in and told us that an American Airlines jetliner had slammed into one of the twin towers.

I grabbed my coat and ran down the marble stairs, passing construction workers, and hurried onto Chambers Street.

Sirens were now splitting the air and there were police lines being set up on Broadway. Several hundred New Yorkers were on the north side of the street gazing up at the World Trade Center. A great gray cloud billowed in slow motion, growing larger and larger, like some evil genie released into the cloudless sky. Twisted hunks of metal were falling off the ruined facade. Sheets of paper fluttered against the grayness like ghostly snowflakes.

Then, at 9:03, there was another boom, and now an immense ball of orange flame exploded out of a high floor of the second tower. "Oh, —, man, oh, —, oh, wow," a man said, backing away, eyes wide with fear and awe, while a few others began running toward the Municipal Building. "No way!" shouted another man. "You believe this?" While a fourth said: "They gotta be dyin' up there."

None of us on that street had seen the second plane coming from the west. Through the clouds of smoke, we couldn't see it smash into the immense tower, loaded with fuel. But there was this expanding, fearful, insidious orange ball: about seven stories high, full of dumb, blind power. For one heart-stopping moment it seemed capable of rolling all the way to where we were standing, charring everything in its path. And then it seemed to sigh and contract, retreating into the building, to burn whatever human beings might still be alive.

CALM & ORDERLY

The odd thing on the street was that so few New Yorkers panicked. The photographs of weeping women and distraught men were exceptions, not the rule. Some stoic New York cool took over. People walked north on Broadway, but few ran. All looked back to see the smoke flowing darkly to the east, toward Brooklyn.

"Go, go, go, go," a police sergeant was shouting, pointing east. And people followed his orders, but didn't grow runny with fear. Now the sky was dark with blacker clouds. Near the corner of Duane Street, two women called to a policewoman: "Officer, officer, where can we go to give blood?" The policewoman said, "I don't know, ma'am, but please keep moving north."

The great stream moved steadily north. My wife and I walked south, gazing up at the beautiful facade of the Woolworth Building, all white and ornate against the clouds of smoke. By now we all knew that this was terrorism; one plane hitting a tower could be an accident, but two were part of a plan. On Vesey Street, outside the Jean Louis David hair salon on the corner of Church Street, we could see a wheel rim from an airplane, guarded by a man in an FBI jacket. Another anonymous hunk of scorched metal was lying on the ground across Vesey Street from St. Paul's, where George Washington once kneeled in prayer.

Near the curb beside the police lines, I could see a puddle of blood already darkening, a woman's black shoe now sticky with blood, an unopened bottle of V-8 Splash, a cheese danish still wrapped in cellophane. Someone had been hurt here, on her way to breakfast at an office desk.

TUMBLING BODIES

But when we looked up, the fires and smoke shifted from ghastly spectacle to specific human horror. It was 9:40. From the north facade of the uptown tower, just below the floor that was spewing orange flame, a human being came flying into the air.

A man.

Shirtless.

Tumbling head over heels at first, until the weight of his torso carried him face-first, story after story, hundreds of feet, in the last terrifying seconds of his life.

We did not see him smash into the ground. He just vanished.

"That's 14 by my count," a cop said. "These poor bastards. . . ."

He didn't finish the sentence. He turned away, talked on a cell phone, hung up, turned to another cop. "Believe this? My mother says they crashed a plane into the—Pentagon!"

The Pentagon? Could that be?

But there was no time to call for details, to see how wide this day would be.

For above us, at 9:55, the first of the towers began to collapse. We heard snap-ping sounds, pops, little explosions, and then the walls bulged out, and we heard a sound like an avalanche, and here it came.

Everything then happened in fragments, scribble. I yell to my wife, "Run!" And we start together, and this immense cloud, perhaps 25 stories high, is rolling at us.

But bodies come smashing together in the doorway of 25 Vesey Street and I can't see my wife, and when I push to get out, I'm driven into the lobby. I keep calling her name, and saying, "I've got to get out of here, please, my wife. . . ."

NO WAY OUT

We're in the building, deep in the lobby, behind walls, and the clear glass doors are gray-brown, locked tight, but the dust whooshes into the lobby. "Don't open that door!" someone says. "Get away from that —— door!" As I write, it remains present tense. We look for a back door. There is none. Joey Newfield, a photographer for the *New York Post,* the son of a close friend, is covered with powder and dust and still making photographs. He is told by a building employee there might be an exit in the basement. A half-dozen of us go down narrow stairs. There is no exit. But there is a water cooler, and we rinse the dust from our mouths.

I'm desperate now to get out, to find my wife, to be sure she's alive, to hug her in the horror. But I'm sealed with these others inside in the tomblike basement of an office building. "Come on, come up

here!" a voice calls, and we start climbing narrow stairs. Back in the lobby, police emergency workers are caked with white powder, coughing, hacking, spitting, like figures from a horror movie. Then there's a sound of splintering glass. One of the emergency workers has smashed open the glass doors. I feel as if I've been there for an hour; only 14 minutes have passed.

"Get going!" a cop yells. "But don't run!"

ASHEN FACES, STREETS

The street before us is now a pale gray wilderness. There is powdery white dust on gutter and sidewalk, and dust on the roofs of cars, and dust on the tombstones of St. Paul's. Dust coats all the walking human beings, the police and the civilians, white people and black, men and women. It's like an assembly of ghosts. Dust has covered the drying puddle of blood and the lone woman's shoe and the

uneaten cheese danish. To the right, the dust cloud is still rising and falling, undulating in a sinister way, billowing out and then falling in upon itself. The tower is gone.

I start running toward Broadway, through dust 2 inches deep. Park Row is white. City Hall Park is white. Sheets of paper are scattered everywhere, orders for stocks, waybills, purchase orders, the pulverized confetti of capitalism. Sirens blare, klaxons wail. I see a black woman with dazed eyes, her hair coated with dust, and an Asian woman masked with powder. I don't see my wife anywhere. I look into store windows. I peer into an ambulance. I ask a cop if there's an emergency center.

"Yeah," he says. "Everywhere."

SEARCHING AMID EXODUS

Then we're all walking north, streams of New Yorkers, thousands of us, holding handkerchiefs to noses, coughing, a few in tears. Many are searching for friends or lovers, husbands or wives. I try a pay phone. Not working. Another. Dead. At Chambers Street, when I look back, City Hall is covered with white powder. So is the dome of the Potter Building on Park Row.

A few more blocks and I'm home, my own face and clothes a ghastly white, and my wife is coming out the door, after checking telephone messages, about to race back into the death-stained city to search for me.

We hug each other for a long time.

All around us, the fine powder of death is falling, put into the New York air by lunatics. Religious war, filled with the melodrama of martyrdom, had come to New York. Almost certainly, it was welded to visions of paradise. And in some ways, on the day of the worst single disaster in New York history, there was a feeling that the dying had only begun. ❚

STEVE HARTMAN | *Correspondent, CBS News:*

IT WAS ALL AT ONCE THE BIGGEST STORY OF MY LIFE and the smallest story of the day. A fourth and final hijacked plane had gone down in a remote field outside Shanksville, Pennsylvania. Eyewitnesses said the plane rocked sharply from side to side just before it crashed and became a huge fireball. But by the time I arrived several hours later there was little left—just the gray haze of a smoldering tire and a giant hole in the ground. United Flight 93 had all but disappeared.

For me, seeing the crash site only added to what was already a baffling mystery. The Pentagon we all understood. The Trade Center seemed a logical target. But a reclaimed strip mine in western Pennsylvania made no sense whatsoever.

Remember, at the time all we knew was that Flight 93 was en route from Newark to San Francisco when it suddenly made a hairpin turn over Cleveland. So using the cardboard cover of my reporter's notebook as a straight edge, I lined up Cleveland and Shanksville on a borrowed road atlas. I then let my finger continue along the projected flight path. The line went through western Maryland. It caught a corner of West Virginia. And as it neared the coast a chill ran down my spine. The plane was heading directly for Washington, D.C.

For the first time it all started to make sense. The eyewitness reports of a plane jerking through the sky. The rumors of a passenger revolt. And now a foiled plot. As I stared at the map, I heard a group of reporters off in the distance debating when and how America would fight back.

A powerful thought welled inside me.

Perhaps we already had.

CYNTHIA BOWERS | *Correspondent, CBS News:*

INTERVIEW WITH LISA JEFFERSON, A GTE AIRFONE SUPERVISOR IN OAK BROOK, ILLINOIS, WHO TOOK UNITED FLIGHT 93 PASSENGER TODD BEAMER'S CALL.

JEFFERSON: When I took the call over, there was a soft-spoken, calm gentleman on the other end. He told me that there were three people that had taken over the flight. At that point, I asked him his name. He told me, "Todd Beamer." He was from Cranbury, New Jersey.

BOWERS: Did you make a conscious decision not to tell Todd about the World Trade Center?

JEFFERSON: Yes.

BOWERS: Why?

JEFFERSON: Because I wanted him to have hope. I wanted him to think that he still had a chance. I didn't want him to feel like it was just totally hopeless and he definitely didn't have a choice and he knew he was going to die. I didn't want him to have that feeling.

BOWERS: When he wanted to pray, was your sense then that . . . that he knew that he was going to die?

JEFFERSON: Yes, I did. I felt that he knew at that time because he had said, "Oh, Jesus, help us." And he said, "Lisa, would you recite the Lord's Prayer with me?" . . . He knew at that time that there wasn't much left for him to do.

BOWERS: What do you think that this country needs to know about the men and women who were on board Flight 93?

JEFFERSON: They're all heroes in my eyes. They really are. They all pitched together and they did what they thought was the best thing to do at that time. And I feel that Todd played a great role in that because when he told the guys, "Are you ready?," I assume that they were waiting on his cue. Then they responded to him, and he said, "Okay, let's roll."

LOS ANGELES 11:24 395 CANCELLED CANCELLED
TUESDAY 10:19 SEPTEMBER 11

9/11/01
8:44 A.M.

ATTN ALL PASSENGERS, ALL FLIGHTS HAVE BEEN
CANCELLED UNTIL FURTHER NOTICE. IF YOU ARE
A CONNECTING PASSENGER'S, PLEASE CONSULT
YOUR AIRLINE IN THE TERMINAL FOR FURTHER
INFORMATION. ALL OTHER PASSENGERS AND
VISITORS PLEASE MAKE ARRANGEMENTS TO
LEAVE THE AIRPORT.

DEPARTMENT OF AVIATION

Destination		Time	Flight	Gate	Status
LOS ANGELES		11:30	55		CANCELLED
LOS ANGELES		12:25	1549		CANCELLED
LOS ANGELE		2:30	31	B42	DELAYED
MANCHESTER	1 STOP	12:41	252		CANCELLED
MCCOOK		1:55	6361		CANCELLED
MEMPHIS		10:30	7979		CANCELLED
MIAMI		12:40	1412	B31	DELAYED
MINNEAPOLIS		12:35	1486		CANCELLED
MOAB		9:25	6701		CANCELLED
MONTROSE		11:25	7125		CANCELLED
NASHVILLE		10:30	5888		CANCELLED
NEW ORLEANS		10:03	1592		CANCELLED
NEW ORLEANS		12:40	1514	B29	DELAYED
NEW YORK LGA		10:12	394	B22	DELAYED
NEW YORK LGA		11:35	412		CANCELLED
NEW YORK LGA		12:35	476		CANCELLED
NEWARK		10:45	422		CANCELLED
NEWARK		12:38	906		CANCELLED
NORFOLK	1 STOP	1:35	6563		CANCELLED

TUESDAY 10:19 SEPTEMBER 11

"Flying Blind: On That Fateful Day, Two Airlines Faced Their Darkest Scenario" [EXCERPT]

by Scott McCartney and Susan Carey, THE WALL STREET JOURNAL, October 15, 2001

Across America, skies were clear, a beautiful day for flying everywhere but in Atlanta, where low clouds draped a summery landscape.

Early in the business day, American Airlines and United Airlines each had more than 100 flights in the air, a fraction of the more than 2,000 flights they each had scheduled. Their top executives were digging through paperwork, meeting with other managers, and answering e-mail from home.

Then, at 7:27 A.M. CDT, Craig Marquis got an emergency phone call.

Mr. Marquis, manager-on-duty at American's sprawling System Operations Control center in Fort Worth, Texas, heard a reservations supervisor explain that an airborne flight attendant, hysterical with fear, was on the phone and needed to talk to the operations center. In the background, Mr. Marquis could hear the flight attendant shrieking and gasping for air.

"She said two flight attendants had been stabbed, one was on oxygen. A passenger had his throat slashed and looked dead, and they [the hijackers] had gotten into the cockpit," Mr. Marquis recalls.

In twenty-two years at American's operations center, Mr. Marquis has made split-second, multimillion-dollar decisions to cancel flights during storms, separate threats from hoaxes, and set in motion the airline's response to a crash. But none of that could have prepared him for the morning of September 11, when all he and other American and United Airlines officials could do was listen and watch as the systems they control spun gruesomely out of control.

"I felt so helpless," says Mr. Marquis. "I was along for the ride."

A little more than twenty minutes later, at United's System Operations Control center in suburban Chicago, Rich "Doc" Miles, the SOC duty manager, received equally startling news: Air-traffic controllers had lost contact with United Flight 175 from Boston to Los Angeles, and a flight attendant on that plane had called in word that the plane had been hijacked. . . .

Jim Goodwin, United's chairman and chief executive, knew instantly that the ramifications went well beyond his airline and American. "The enormity of this is going to change everyone's life profoundly," he recalls thinking to himself.

As American and United lost communications, one by one, with a total of four hijacked planes, confusion set in. Managers couldn't tell right away which particular plane had been ensnared in the catastrophes that unfolded on TV sets all around them. There was an unprecedented flurry of intercompany calls; even the two chief executives spoke by phone.

Quickly, people at the football-field-size command centers began executing the biggest shutdown in commercial aviation's eighty-year history, orders that preempted even the Federal Aviation Administration's grounding of planes and may have prevented other hijackings. Beyond that, UAL Corp.'s United and AMR Corp.'s American also had to attend to victims' relatives, secure hundreds of stranded airplanes, and accommodate tens of thousands of stranded passengers and crew.

"I remember thinking, I'm in one of those B-movies, with a script so bizarre no one would believe it. It cannot be happening," says Donald J. Carty, American's chairman and chief executive officer.

Sitting in the middle of a horseshoe of desks surrounded by screens, phones, and computers when his hotline began blinking, Mr. Marquis didn't have time to imagine the unimaginable that was about to take place. Calm and quick-thinking, he told others in the operations center of the call he'd just received from a woman who identified herself as Betty Ong, an at-

tendant aboard Flight 11, a Boeing 767 wide-body that had left Boston thirty minutes earlier. Fearing a hoax, he called up her personnel record and asked her to verify her employee number and nickname.

She did. This was real.

"Is there a doctor on board?" Mr. Marquis remembers asking.

"No. No doctor," Ms. Ong said.

The plane had been headed to Los Angeles, but it turned south over Albany, New York, and began flying erratically, most likely when hijackers were killing the plane's two pilots. FAA air-traffic controllers told American's operation center that they could hear arguing over the plane's radio. Ms. Ong, screaming but still coherent, said the four hijackers had come from first-class seats 2A, 2B, 9A, and 9B. The fatally injured passenger was in 10B. The hijackers had hit people with some sort of spray that made her eyes burn. She was having trouble breathing, Mr. Marquis recalls her saying.

"Is the plane descending?" Mr. Marquis asked.

"We're starting to descend," Ms. Ong said. "We're starting to descend."

Air-traffic controllers couldn't get a response to frantic voice and text messages to the cockpit. Hijackers had turned off the plane's transponder, which identifies an airplane among hundreds of other blips on a radar, but Mr. Marquis had an aide tell the FAA that American had confirmed a hijacking.

"They're going to New York!" Mr. Marquis remembers shouting out. "Call Newark and JFK and tell them to expect a hijacking," he ordered, assuming the hijackers would land the plane. "In my wildest dreams, I was not thinking the plane was going to run into a building," Mr. Marquis says.

Even as the line to Flight 11 was still open, American's executives were rushing to the operations center to deal with the crisis. Gerard Arpey, American's executive vice president of operations, had been in Boston the day before for his grandmother's funeral, and had arrived at his desk in Fort Worth at 7:15 A.M. CDT to work through a pile of issues that needed attention. The forty-three-year-old executive called American's operations center to say he couldn't participate in the daily 7:45 A.M. system-wide operations call.

Joe Bertapelle, the manager at American's operations center, told him of Ms. Ong's phone call that had just come in. Mr. Arpey slumped back in his chair and sat stunned for thirty seconds. "Something inside me said this had the ring of truth to it," Mr. Arpey recalls. He called the office of Mr. Carty, who was at home answering e-mails, and left word of a possible hijacking, then hurried to the operations center a few miles west.

As he walked in, he was met immediately by Mr. Bertapelle and Craig Parfitt, manager of American's dispatch operations, a twenty-nine-year American veteran nicknamed "Ice Man" for his even

keel. Mr. Marquis had confirmed the hijacking, they told Mr. Arpey, and they had to open American's crisis command center, a room perched one floor up in the operations center. The facility is used in the event of crashes, military troop movements, and other emergencies.

A page went out to American's top executives and operations personnel: "Confirmed hijacking Flight 11." The regular 7:45 CDT conference call started, but was almost immediately interrupted: "Gentlemen, I have some information here I need to relay," Mr. Bertapelle announced.

The FAA had tagged the radar blip that Flight 11 had become, and it was now isolated on an Aircraft Situation Display, a big radar-tracking screen. All eyes watched as the plane headed south. On the screen, the plane showed a squiggly line after its turn near Albany, then it straightened. "All we knew for sure was that he's not going to LAX," said Mr. Bertapelle.

Big centers deal almost daily with unusual events, from bomb scares to blizzards to unruly passengers, and they hold frequent crisis drills. In those few minutes of uncertainty, American's operations experts were trying to anticipate the plane's next move. But they were in new territory here.

At 7:48 A.M. CDT, the radar image stopped moving and showed Flight 11 "frozen" over New York. A blink more, the plane simply vanished from the screen.

Three minutes later, a ramp supervisor

at Kennedy airport in New York called to say a plane had flown into a World Trade Center tower....

Mr. Arpey was on the phone with Mr. Carty. "The press is reporting an airplane hit the World Trade Center. Is that our plane?" Mr. Carty remembers asking.

"I don't know, Don. We confirmed it was hijacked, and was headed south from Boston," Mr. Arpey told him.

Mr. Carty had a bad feeling that it was indeed his plane that had hit the north tower. But when his wife asked him point blank, he replied, "No, it couldn't be.... In my brain, I knew. But I couldn't say it," Mr. Carty recalls.

Outside Chicago, at United's SOC, Mike Barber, the dispatch manager, had his eye on a large overhead screen that happened to be tuned to CNN. "My God, the World Trade Center's on fire," Mr. Barber remembers blurting out.

Bill Roy, United's SOC director, wheeled to look at the pictures. "It looks like a small airplane," he said to the others. "Maybe they veered off the La Guardia flight path?" But within minutes, United got a call from the FAA saying it was an American Airlines jet.

Mr. Roy called over to the adjacent headquarters building, where Mr. Goodwin, United's chairman and chief executive, was having his morning session with senior officers. Today, he was sitting with Andy Studdert, forty-five, the chief operating officer; Rono Dutta, United's president, and three or four others.

Maryann Irving, Mr. Studdert's secretary, took Mr. Roy's call and ran to Mr. Goodwin's second-floor office, knocked, and burst into the room. "Andy," she said, "call the SOC. An American plane just went into the World Trade Center."

Mr. Goodwin remembers thinking, "This is rather bizarre," and flipped on the TV.

Mr. Studdert, a former banker who joined United only six years ago, ran across the bridge between the two buildings and entered the SOC, thinking about American: "My God, what are they going to go through?" Upon reaching the command post, he barked out, "Confirm—American into World Trade Center."

A manager at the post had other news: "Boss, we've lost contact with one of our airplanes."

A few minutes later, Doc Miles, the SOC shift manager, heard from United's maintenance center in San Francisco, which has a system to take in-flight calls from flight attendants about cabin items that need repairs. The mechanic had gotten a call from a female flight attendant on Flight 175, who had said, "Oh, my God, the crew has been killed, a flight attendant has been stabbed. We've been hijacked." Then, the line from the plane went dead.

"No, the information we're getting is that it was an American 757," Mr. Miles recalls protesting.

The mechanic insisted, "No, we got a call from a flight attendant on 175."

The dispatcher monitoring Flight 175, a Boeing 767 from Boston to Los Angeles, sent messages by radio and to the cockpit computer, and got no response. At 8:03 CDT, the group—now assembling in the crisis room off the SOC under Mr. Studdert's command—watched as a large, dark jet slammed into the second tower of the World Trade Center.

While United was trying to understand what happened to Flight 175, American's operations experts received a call from the FAA saying that a second American plane, Flight 77 out of Washington-Dulles, had turned off its transponder and turned around. Controllers had lost radio communications with the plane. Without hearing from anyone on the plane, American didn't know its location.

That raised the disaster to a whole new level. Mr. Arpey looked across the crisis room at Ralph Richardi, a vice president in charge of operations planning, and saw his eyes widen in horror. "That was the first time we realized this was something other than a hijacking," Mr. Richardi says.

Mr. Arpey instantly gave an order to ground every American plane in the Northeast that hadn't yet taken off. Within minutes, American got word that United also had an airliner missing and out of contact.

"The minute we heard that, we all agreed we needed to ground-stop the whole airline," Mr. Arpey said. At 8:15 A.M. CDT, the order went out on the command center's loudspeaker: No new take-offs. The decision, though it clearly would lead to monstrous logistical headaches, could save lives. "I never sensed any fear or panic. We were too shell-shocked," says Mr. Arpey.

Meanwhile, United was making similar decisions. Mr. Studdert ordered all international flights frozen on the ground at 8:20. Ten minutes later, United began diverting its domestic flights and putting them on the ground.

Just as these orders were being given, the American command center heard television reports of a plane hitting the south tower of the trade center. Many in the room instantly assumed it was American Flight 77, the missing plane from Washington.

"How did 77 get to New York and we didn't know it?" Mr. Bertapelle recalls shouting.

Mr. Arpey looked at Mr. Carty, who had just arrived. "I said, 'I think we better get everything on the deck'" and shut down the whole airline.

Mr. Carty replied, "Do it."

American ordered planes to land at the nearest suitable airport. It activated crash teams to deal with the accidents and the families of passengers and began beefing up security at American's headquarters and major stations. Mr. Carty called his counterpart at United, Mr. Goodwin. Each man told the other he thought he had a second missing plane. "We focused entirely on what was transpiring—the physical takeover of our planes," recalls Mr. Goodwin.

Mr. Carty and Mr. Goodwin also were talking on the phone with Secretary of Transportation Norman Mineta, who was in a government command bunker with Vice President Dick Cheney. Mr. Carty told Mr. Mineta that American was ordering all 162 of its planes out of the sky; United already had ordered its 122 planes down. About five minutes later, the FAA shut down the skies over the U.S. completely to all but military aircraft.

At 8:45 A.M. CDT, American lost contact with a third flight, a Boston-to-Seattle trip. Everyone in the room was convinced it was a third hijacking. But it turned out to be a radio glitch, and the panic ended when radio contact was restored in ten minutes.

Soon, reports began pouring in that a plane had crashed into the Pentagon. Maybe it was the missing United plane? American still believed its Flight 77 had gone into the second World Trade Center tower. The command center ordered a plane readied to take crisis response teams to New York to assist investigators and relatives of passengers.

Captain Ed Soliday, United's vice president of safety and security, talked to AMR [AMR Corp., American's parent company] Vice Chairman Bob Baker trying to sort out the confusion. "We did not want to mislead families and loved ones," said Captain Soliday. "American was really pressing us. They thought our airplane had crashed in Washington, and that both their planes had crashed at the World Trade Center. We weren't sure." Finally, he and Mr. Baker agreed the government should make the final confirmation.

Mr. Carty recalls quizzing Mr. Mineta for confirmation of which plane had hit the Pentagon. "I was frustrated. I remember saying, 'For God's sake, it's in the Pentagon. Can't somebody go look at it and see whose plane it is?' "

"They have," Mr. Mineta responded, according to Mr. Carty's recollection. The problem, Mr. Mineta told him: "You can't tell."

At about 8:30 CDT, air-traffic controllers and United lost contact with United Flight 93, a 757 bound from Newark to San Francisco. The dispatcher who had handled Flight 175 had been sending messages to all thirteen of his assigned flights that were airborne, instructing them to land at the nearest United station because of two World Trade Center crashes. One flight didn't answer: Flight 93.

The dispatcher, a forty-two-year veteran of United .... kept firing off messages, but there was no response.

In the United crisis center, managers isolated Flight 93 on the big Aircraft Situation Display screen. The plane had made a wide U-turn over Ohio and seemed to be heading toward Washington. Everyone in the room by now knew that a flight attendant on board had called the mechanics' desk to report that one hijacker had a bomb strapped on and another was holding a knife on the crew. There also were

reports that passengers were calling their families from cell phones and seatback air phones.

"This was worse because we watched it until the end of the radar track . . . and then, poof," says Mr. Roy, director of system operations control. "We didn't have time to cry." That was at 9:03 A.M. CDT.

After Flight 93 crashed, Mr. Studdert dispatched Pete McDonald, United's senior vice president of airport services, to Pennsylvania. Mr. McDonald had himself been in the air on a flight that was diverted from Washington's National Airport to Dulles. Because the no-fly order made flying to the crash site uncertain, Mr. McDonald recruited forty United volunteers at Dulles, all trained in humanitarian relief duties, rounded up eight vans and cars, and set off at noon. In Pennsylvania, two state trooper squad cars met the caravan to give it a speedy escort.

After reaching the site, Mr. McDonald went up in a helicopter to take a look and all he could see was "very small pieces" of debris, since the plane itself was deep in the trench it created when it crashed.

With each twist and turn, airline officials also had the grisly task of trying to understand who was on board and who the hijackers were. Early on, American officials pulled up computerized passenger lists from Flights 11 and 77. With seat numbers from their flight attendant's call, they quickly identified suspects. United, working with the FBI, did the same. Other Middle Eastern names jumped out,

and as calls poured in from worried relatives, they quickly realized that they hadn't gotten calls for those very passengers.

The tally: 19 suspected hijackers, 213 passengers, 8 pilots, and 25 flight attendants.

Within two hours, all of United's and American's domestic flights were on the ground and accounted for. Late in the afternoon, however, United still had some planes over the Pacific. These were nerve-racking times. United said it had to press hard on Canadian authorities and even Alaskan airport officials who initially refused to let the planes land. "Until we got the last airplanes on the ground, we were biting our fingers," CEO Mr. Goodwin recalls. "By then, we were spooked. Every time we got an unusual communication from an airplane, we thought, 'My God, is there another one?' "

Once all planes were safely on the ground, the airlines sat stunned at the logistical quagmire before them. They would have to figure out where each of their hundreds of planes were and how to get tens of thousands of stranded passengers back to their destinations. They had to instantly create new security procedures. The days would turn into a blur of conference calls to regulators. Plans constantly changed. There was no time to go home and watch TV reports, no time to reflect.

For many in the command center that day, grief was delayed for days, if not weeks, by the workload. "Some of the reality of what happened both to our country and our company didn't set in until much later," says Mr. Arpey, who stayed in the crisis center all through the night.

For most, going home brought the first real emotional shock. "It hit me when I first looked in my kids' faces," pictures of shock and sorrow, says Kyle Phelps, manager of administration for the operations center and a twenty-seven-year veteran with American.

Mr. Parfitt, the "Ice Man," says it didn't hit him until much later, when he began to realize that his son in the army might be headed to war. "The grief for the people on the airplanes, for the crews, for the people of New York in the World Trade Center is all-encompassing," Mr. Parfitt says.

Mr. Bertapelle says that when he is home now he craves the Comedy Channel, hungry for a laugh. On the Friday after the hijacking, Mr. Carty came on American's intercom system, piped through its headquarters, operations center, flight academy, and other facilities, to observe a moment of silence. "That's the first time I remember just stopping to think about it," Mr. Bertapelle said. "Any moment of silence is hell." . . .

Mr. Studdert, United's chief operating officer, got a call three days after the terrorist attacks from an old friend. "How you doing, kid?" the friend asked. "There is no kid left in me anymore," Mr. Studdert replied. "I'll never be the same person. We'll never be the same company or the same country." ‖

CAROL MARIN [IN CBS NEWS STUDIO STILL COVERED WITH DUST AND PIECES OF DEBRIS]: Dan, I think I was in the second collapse. I was coming toward the World Trade Center, looking for CBS crews, and asked a firefighter if he saw any. He told me to walk down the middle of the road. All of a sudden, there was a roar, an explosion, and we could see coming toward us a ball of flame, stories high. He, and others, screamed, "Run." And I ran. I fell. One of the firefighters picked me up. We ran as fast as we could. And then he threw me into the wall of a building and covered me. I'm in his debt. You know, Dan, I know firefighters do incredible work all of the time, but this exceeded anything I can imagine. He threw me into a wall, covered me with his body. I could feel his heart banging against my back, we were both so sure we were going to die.

The flame somehow stopped short of us. But whatever collapsed created a rain of cinders so thick you couldn't see in front of you. And you couldn't breathe. A police officer . . . grabbed my hand and he and I tried to find our way through it [the smoke]. Again, we thought we were finished. We somehow got to the light. Another firefighter gave me his mask for a moment so I could breathe. And then I made my way somehow through the smoke, into the light, to our crews.

There was a cameraman there whose head was bloody, and he was trying to shoot and set up some shots. People streamed toward me as I made my way back to the Trade Center, sobbing and crying and trying to call home on cell phones, but they couldn't get through.

... And then a New York City bus driver opened the doors of his empty bus and drove me here to the broadcast center. The citizens of New York have remained amazingly calm, but deeply frightened.

A Widow's Walk

By Marian Fontana

"*On September 11th, I dropped my son off at his second full day of kindergarten. The sky was so smooth and blue it looked as if it had been ironed. I crossed Seventh Avenue and ordered coffee. The benches outside were already filled with Park Slope mothers perched behind Maclaren strollers. I sat to wait for my husband to meet me. It was our eighth wedding anniversary and Dave and I were about to begin a new chapter in our seventeen years together. Sipping coffee, I watched as a line of thick black smoke crept across the sky from Manhattan, oblivious to the fact that my life was about to change forever.*"

My eyes creak open and try to read the red numbers that blink 8:25 A.M. A surge of panic rushes through me as I realize I am late for Aidan's second day of kindergarten. I should have laid out his clothes and packed his lunch the night before, but the organizational gene is recessive in my family, and so I scramble to find Aidan a shirt.

"Wake up!" I yell, glancing at my five-year-old son sleeping in the bottom bunk. His mouth hangs wide and his cheeks are flush like the red sheen of tempera paint. I watch the soothing rhythm of his chest rise and fall and I stop to fill my own lungs with gratefulness.

"C'mon! We're late!"

Aidan stirs and I rush into the kitchen to make lunch and call Dave at the firehouse on Union Street, only eight blocks away. Last night we tried to have our usual eleven o'clock phone call, but the squad's PA system had been broken. Everything was accompanied by a deafening sound resembling a bee caught in a microphone.

"I can't talk," he had said. "This noise is driving me crazy."

"Ten more hours and you'll be on vacation for a month," I reminded him.

He wasn't supposed to work last night, but I had insisted he switch his shifts to be off for our anniversary.

Like a weary senior, Aidan shuffles into the kitchen and sinks into a chair. "I'm tired," he complains, plopping his head onto his folded arms.

I kiss his hair, inhaling the scent of sweat and baby shampoo. I dial the firehouse and squeeze the phone to my ear. Dave answers.

"Hey. . . happy anniversary," I say.

"You too." He sounds exhausted. He has been working double time to pay back shifts he borrowed for our vacation in Cape Cod. Smearing peanut butter on potato bread, I ask him when he will finish.

"I just have to shower," he answers. I picture him grimy and smelling of smoke. No matter how many times he shampoos,

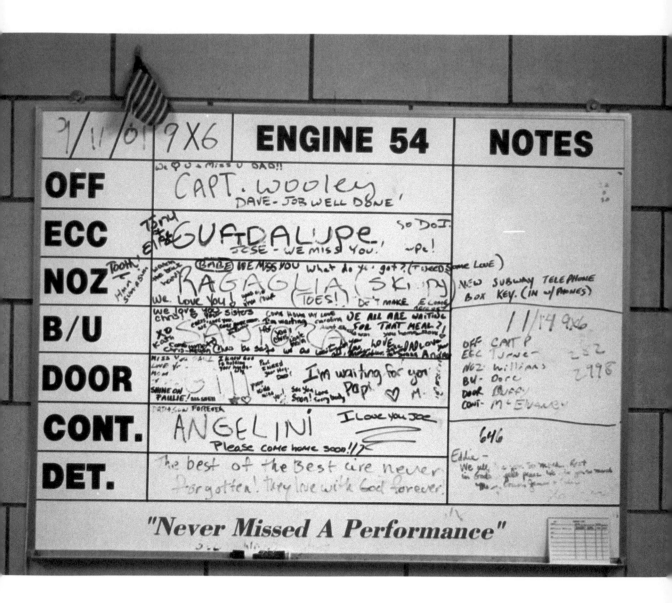

his hair, skin, and clothes always smell like the bottom of a fireplace.

"Are you sure you're done?" I ask hurriedly, scanning the shelf for jelly. Since Dave is the only firefighter who lives in the neighborhood, he is often the last to go because his "commute" is so short. Despite my protests, he often remains so the other firefighters can begin their commutes to Long Island, Rockaway, and Staten Island.

"I'm done," he answers, and I can tell he is as excited as I am. My neck hurts from squeezing the phone and Aidan is asking me for a waffle.

"I'm late. Where do you want to meet?"

"How about the muffin store in ten minutes?" he suggests. I can hear the firemen in the background.

"Fine," I say pulling the jelly that's stuck on the refrigerator shelf, and I hang up. That's it. No profound discussions. No passionate good-byes. I can't even remember if I told him I loved him. We always did, but even habits you forget sometimes, like turning off the coffeepot or locking the door.

By 8:36 A.M. I drag Aidan outside with a squeeze yogurt hanging from his mouth. There was no time for waffles, and now I guiltily rush him down Seventh Avenue.

Bill Deblasio, my friend and a candidate for city council, is shaking voters' hands. Fresh-faced college students hand out flyers. I try to get Aidan to walk faster, but he drags behind me like luggage.

"Can we get an Anakin Skywalker toy after school?" His little hand is warm and clammy, and even on busy days, I enjoy how it feels.

"Uncle Jason is picking you up."

"How come?"

"It's Daddy's and my anniversary today."

"Are you going to have a party?"

"No. We're going out in the big city."

"Can I come?"

"No. You have school."

"Can Jason buy me Anakin?"

If Aidan were a dog, he would be a retriever. I convince myself that his obsessive single-mindedness will serve him well someday as we cross the playground to the school door.

The kindergarten room is noisy and stifling. Aidan bounces toward his seat, oblivious to the little girl next to him crying noisily and clutching her father's pants leg. I kiss Aidan good-bye on the top of his head. His hair is so soft it feels like a new, cool cotton pillow.

"I love you," I say.

"Love you too," he answers distractedly.

I walk outside and peek in the window. A few more children are crying, but Aidan is talking to a curly-headed boy next to him. His fact is expressive and sincere and I watch his eyebrows bounce up and down like caterpillars dancing.

I remind myself to vote and smile with guilty pleasure at having the day alone with Dave. With Aidan finally attending school all day, we can begin to balance the tray of family, friends, exercise, sex, and errands without its crashing to the floor.

The air is warm and lingers with the smell of summer. Leaning on a white Volvo, my friend Catherine waves at me. Catherine speaks as crisp as the sky and fills her sentences with words I have to look up in a dictionary.

"I'm so glad I ran into you!" Her wide cheeks spread into a smile. "I'm leaving for the Congo on Friday and I wanted to have a chance to see you."

Catherine is a former member of my writing group; she wrote elegant travel essays. While I spent my teens poured into Sassoon jeans and shopping at the Staten Island Mall, Catherine contemplated the evils of apartheid in the dirt back roads of Zimbabwe.

"What have you been up to?! I never see you anymore." She grabs my arms.

"I don't know what happens to my days. I feel like I wake up, take a breath, and it's bedtime."

Catherine closes her deep-set eyes and nods in tacit agreement. I ask her about her upcoming trip, for which she has been hired to write about gorilla poachers.

"I'm a bit nervous about my photographer. I find him very likable, but he has a reputation for being an obstreperous traveler."

I envy the exotic writing assignments Catherine gets but know that I am not capable of such high adventure. Performing and writing about the curious urban characters I witness on the F train is as about

as intrepid as I want to be. I suddenly realize that I am late to meet Dave, and jog into Connecticut Muffin. I am surprised when I see that Dave isn't there. Behind the counter, Bobby hands me my coffee before I even have to ask for it. He is a soft-spoken, tall African man in his late fifties. I always tease him about smoking too much and he shakes his head and chuckles, his laugh as smooth as my coffee.

Outside people are talking animatedly. I hear the word "airplane" and "Twin Towers" when Lori walks over. She is a short, blond ex-dancer with two wild boys and a face that's seen too much sun. She teaches aerobics at the dance studio where I used to teach gymnastics.

"A plane just crashed into the Twin Towers." People begin pointed at a plume of smoke cutting across the blue sky like a black arrow. I picture a small biplane wedged into the top of the tower, like a candle pushed onto a cake. I convince myself that Dave could miss a big job. After all, it's our anniversary, and he must be home. He probably wants to fool around before we head to the city.

"Where are you going?" Lori asks concerned.

"I think Dave might be waiting for me at home." Dave hated that I was always late. Having taught in the neighborhood for eight years, I could never make it down the avenue without stopping to talk to parents, kids, and friends. Dave dubbed me "Pope of the Slope," and we

KEEP-BACK-300

often avoided Seventh Avenue so we could get places on time.

People are looking up over the horizon toward Manhattan. Another thick black plume of smoke joins the first.

"Let me come with you," Lori insists and she follows me down the brownstone steps into my small apartment.

"Dave?" I yell down the hall, but everything is eerily quiet. Lori turns on the television, and I am stunned to see the whole top of the tower engulfed in flames like a giant metal matchstick. My heart beats fast as I notice the second tower is also on fire. Footage of a plane crashing into the second tower plays, and I am confused. It this a stunt, or some kind of camera trick?

My breath catches in my throat as I watch people jump from windows, falling like ash. A man in a green shirt tucks his knees up, like a kid doing a cannonball into a pool and jumps. The voices on the news sound confused and frightened as they flash to the Pentagon, which is also in flames. The television cuts back to the towers. A man uses his white shirt like a parachute and jumps from the roof. I cup my hand over my mouth, trying to stop the shock of what I'm seeing. Lori is talking, but all I can hear is my heart pounding in my ears. The shaky voices on the news report a crash in Philadelphia and planes all over the country with strangers in the cockpits. I know it is the apocalypse. It is the end of the world.

"What is happening?" I ask the television. Everything sounds muffled as if I'm underwater or under a pillow. My phone rings but sounds far away. Thank goodness. Dave is calling, explaining to me what is happening to the world.

"Marian, please tell me Dave is with you."

It is Mila, my friend from college who lives in the neighborhood.

"He's working, I think." I imagine him running, his tired legs carrying a hundred pounds of equipment, the heat from the tower banking down like a heavy blanket.

"What would he be doing there?" Mila asks, my worry swelling in my chest.

"He'd be running in, I think . . . up the steps . . . to save people—"

I watch the South Tower fall. Gray spires pour out like fireworks of dust, ash, and metal as I drop the phone. The ventricles of my heart start to pulse and expand, ripping and exploding in my chest. I clutch my heart, but it is as futile as trying to stop the ocean.

"Oh my God. He's dead. He's gone," I scream, sinking into the rug.

"No. You don't know that," Lori says helplessly.

"I'm sure he's fine. He's probably helping people," she continues.

But I know. I would be asked about this moment again and again for weeks and months after. On a sunny September morning, the chord that connected my heart to Dave's was severed, ripped like a plug from its socket, and I knew he was gone. ∎

next report, I heard metallic crashes and looked up out of the office window to see what seemed like perfectly synchronized explosions coming from each floor, spewing glass and metal outward. One after the other, from top to bottom, with a fraction of a second between, the floors blew to pieces. It was the building apparently collapsing in on itself, pancaking to the earth.

This was too close. Uncertain whether the building would now fall on ours, I dove under a desk. The windows were pelted by debris, apparently breaking—I'd never know for sure. The room filled with ash, concrete dust, smoke, the detritus of South Tower. It was choking, and as more debris rained down onto and into the building, the light of the day disappeared. I crawled on the floor and braced myself under a desk deeper in the office. But the air was as bad.

With my shirt now over my mouth in the blackout of the smoke, unable to do more than squint because of the stinging ash, and thinking that this is what it must be like on the upper floors of the Towers, I realized I had to move. I stood up from under the desk and began feeling the wall and desks, trying to orient myself in the now pitch-black cubicled world of our modern office. Disoriented, I twice passed by the entryway to this particular corner of the ninth floor. And then I was through, by accident, into a larger space, with more air.

The smoke had spread over the entire floor, which had been evacuated minutes before. In the emergency stairwell, still thinking that it was a matter of time before our building was crushed, I breathed in my first clear air. At ground level, though, it was a different story.

Outside on the sidewalk, the scene looked like Pompeii after the eruption of Mount Vesuvius. Inches of ash on the ground. Smoke and dust clouding the air. My throat stung as I worked my way past ambulances and EMS workers who had been caught outside when the tower collapsed. The emergency workers were trying to find colleagues. In the silence, as the ash fell like snow, radios crackled: "Steve, Steve, where are you?"

One fireman bashed through a door of a diner, and a handful of us took refuge from the outside air. We opened the restaurant's cooler, distributed water bottles, and took some outside to give to the ambulances. I asked what had happened to the people evacuated from the buildings, my colleagues. Did they get away? No one knew.

I stepped into one ambulance with water and asked for a surgical face mask. I was handed several, and later passed them to coughing, spitting emergency workers in the street. The mask would be my life saver.

Because as I walked down the street, getting my bearings, and moving closer to Liberty Street, which opened out onto the

Trade Center compound, the second tower was weakening. I heard a pressing metallic roar, like the Chicago El rumbling overhead. And then the fireman next to me shouted, "It's coming down! Run!"

Run where? I had no idea, so I did the best thing at the moment: I ran after the fireman.

Four of his colleagues joined us, plus another civilian or two on the street. We sprinted behind the wall of a nearby apartment building as the North Tower collapsed two blocks away. "Stay away from glass windows!" he shouted as we ran, but what he said next was drowned out by the roar passing right through us. We flattened ourselves against a metal doorway, this small group, trying to be one with the building, as chunks of concrete and metal fell from the sky behind us and roared up the street and into the building's courtyard all around us. Debris fell against the shirt on my left shoulder— I couldn't push it any harder against the building.

After two minutes, we all went down, in a collective crouch, and tried to breathe. The building had stopped falling. The

roar had subsided. But the smoke and ash seemed as dense as tar, far worse than in the building when the first tower fell. We all were wearing the tight-fitting surgical masks which, with shirts pulled up over our faces, made the difference.

Hyperventilating from the sprint and the fear, the group concentrated on not panicking. Our leader, the fireman who warned of the glass, yelled out in the dark, "Is anybody hurt? Try to breathe through your nose!"

In the blackness, he tried his radio: "Mike! Mike! Where are you?" No answer. Again, and no answer. My hand was on his trembling back, the better to brace myself, and I thought about asking him how long these blackouts and ash clouds could last. Then I realized the full ridiculousness of the question. How would he know? How often does a 110-story building collapse to the ground? I honestly wondered whether I'd survive long enough for the air to clear.

Mike finally answered the radio and was wearing a respirator. He also had a flashlight. And so eventually he found us. Blinded by the ash in our eyes, we stood up as a line, each put a hand on the shoulder of the guy in front, and let Mike lead us out of the darkness into the lobby of a building twenty steps away.

We poured water into our eyes, and shook ash from our clothing and hair. I looked for Mike to thank him, but he had already left to help an injured EMS worker on the street.

A young man in the lobby, apparently missed in the evacuation, held his daughter, a little blond-haired girl perhaps two years old. She was crying. An older man who had also sought shelter was raving uncontrollably nearby. We calmed the older man, and the girl stopped crying. ‖

PAMELA McCALL | *CBS Radio News Correspondent:*

IT IS A SCENE OF UTTER DEVASTATION BEFORE MY EYES. The second World Trade Center Tower is demolishing. People are screaming in the streets here in utter disbelief, clutching their heads. There are plenty of tears. People cannot believe that these towers have come down.

I've seen a lot of people running for their lives. The people who get to this point are very tired, about half a mile away, and they can't believe they are lucky enough to have gotten out of there. A lot of people heard one explosion, ran outside or looked out their windows and saw the aircraft crash into the tower. They immediately tried to get out of the area as best they could, especially before one of the towers collapsed, or a good portion of it. The devastation that is before us right now is unbelievable in terms of an entire World Trade Tower collapsing. There's nothing left of this thing. All we see is a calm billow of smoke, which marks where this building once stood.

I'm standing here watching ambulances go by. They're covered in about three inches of soot and ashes. It resembles the scene of a volcanic eruption with firemen and emergency personnel now donning face masks so they can breathe. I'm looking down at the sight of what used to be the World Trade Center towers. They're both gone.

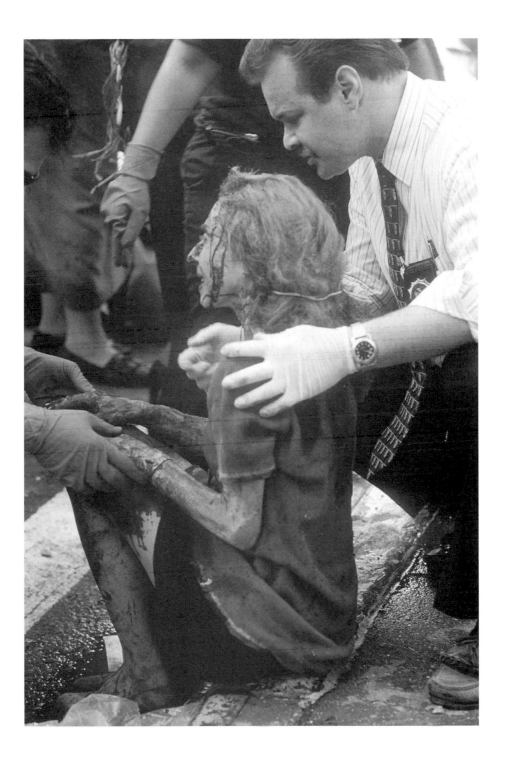

"The Way Down"

by Michael Wright with Cal Fussman, ESQUIRE

At 8:48 on the morning of September 11, Michael Wright was a thirty-year-old account executive working on the eighty-first floor of the World Trade Center. Two hours later, he was something else. This is his story of his escape.

Up to that day, I'd had a Brady Bunch, cookie-cutter, beautiful life. I now know what it's like to have a 110-story building that's been hit by a 767 come down on my head. For better or for worse, it's part of my life. There are things I never thought I'd know that I now know.

It was as mundane a morning as you can imagine. Tuesdays are usually the days I go out to see clients and make sales calls. I get to my office at a quarter to eight, eat a bran muffin, drink a cup of coffee, and get my head straight for the day.

I was actually in a good mood. A couple of us were yukking it up in the men's room. We'd just started sharing the eighty-first floor of 1 World Trade Center with Bank of America, and they'd put up a sign telling everyone to keep the bathroom clean. "Look at this," one of us said. "They move in and now they're giving us shit." It was about quarter to nine.

All of a sudden, there was the shift of an earthquake. People ask, "Did you hear a boom?" No. The way I can best describe it is that every joint in the building jolted.

You ever been in a big old house when a gust of wind comes through and you hear all the posts creak? Picture that creaking being not a matter of inches but of feet. We all got knocked off balance. One guy burst out of a stall buttoning up his pants, saying, "What the fuck?" The flex caused the marble walls in the bathroom to crack.

You're thinking, Gas main. It was so percussive, so close. I opened the bathroom door, looked outside, and saw fire.

There was screaming. One of my coworkers, Alicia, was trapped in the women's room next door. The doorjamb had folded in on itself and sealed the door shut. This guy Art and another guy started kicking the shit out of the door, and they finally got her out.

There was a huge crack in the floor of the hallway that was about half a football field long, and the elevator bank by my office was completely blown out. If I'd walked over, I could've looked all the way down. Chunks of material that had been part of the wall were in flames all over the floor. Smoke was everywhere.

I knew where the stairs were because a couple of guys from my office used to smoke butts there. I started screaming, "Out! Out! Out!" The managers were trying to keep people calm and orderly, and here I was screaming, "The stairs! The stairs!"

We got to the stairwell, and people were in various states. Some were in shock; some were crying. We started filing down in two rows, fire-drill style. I'd left my cell phone at my desk, but my coworkers had theirs. I tried my wife twenty times but couldn't get through. Jenny had gone up to Boston with her mother and grandmother and was staying with my family. Our son was with her. Ben's six months old. It was impossible to reach them.

The thing that kept us calm on the stairs was the thought that what happened couldn't possibly happen. The building could not come down. After a while, as we made our way down, we started to lighten up. Yeah, we knew something bad had happened, but a fire doesn't worry you as much when you're thirty floors below it. I even made an off-color joke to my buddy Ryan. The intent was for only Ryan to hear, but things quieted down just as I said it, so everyone heard. I said, "Ryan, hold me."

He said, "Mike . . . I didn't know."

I said, "Well, we're all going to die, might as well tell you."

Some people were laughing, but not the guy in front of me. "I really think you should keep that humor down!" he said. I felt lousy. In hindsight, he may have known more than I did. Even though I'd seen physical damage, what I can't stress enough is how naïve I was at that point.

Some floors we'd cruise down; others we'd wait for ten minutes. People were speculating, "Was it a bomb?" But we were all getting out. I didn't think I was going to die.

At the fortieth floor, we started coming in contact with firemen. They were saying, "C'mon, down you go! Don't worry, it's safe below." Most of them were stone-faced. Looking back, there were some frightened firemen.

When we got below the thirtieth floor, they started to bring down injured people from flights above. There was a guy with the back of his shirt burned off, a little burn on his shoulder. One woman had severe burns on her face.

We got down to the twentieth floor and a fireman said, "Does anyone know CPR?" I'm no longer certified, but I know it from college. That was ten years ago. You wouldn't want me on an EMT team, but if it comes down to saving somebody, I know how.

So me and this other guy volunteer. We helped this one heavy, older man who came down huffing and puffing, and we kept our eyes out for anyone else. "Do you need help? Do you need help?" Nobody needed help. The stairway became wide-open. It was time to go. The other guy took off in front of me. We were going pretty fast.

Have you ever been to the World Trade Center? There's a mezzanine level; then you go downstairs, which is subterranean, into this big mall. Our stairwell exited out onto that mezzanine level. At that point, I could look out across the plaza at 2 World Trade

Center. That's when I realized the gravity of what had happened. I saw dead bodies everywhere, and none that I saw were intact. It was hard to tell how many. Fifty, maybe? I remember my hand coming up in front of my face to block the sight. Then I took off. As I ran, people were coming out of another stairwell. I stopped and said, "Don't look outside! Don't look outside!" The windows were stained with blood. Someone who'd jumped had fallen very close to the building.

It felt like my head was going to blow up.

I made it to the stairwell and got down. The mall was in bad shape. It must have been from chunks of the plane coming down. Windows were smashed. Sprinklers were on.

I saw Alicia, the coworker who'd been trapped in the bathroom. She'd seen what I'd seen in the plaza and was traumatized. She was crying and moving slowly. I put my arm around her. Then there was another woman—same thing. I put my arm around the two of them, saying, "C'mon. We gotta go. We gotta go."

We were moving through the mall toward the escalator that would take us back up to street level and out to Church Street. There were some emergency workers giving us the "head this way" sign. I think they were trying to get us as far

away from the fire as possible and out toward Church Street and the Millenium Hilton hotel.

I got to the bottom of the escalator, and that's when I heard what sounded like a crack. That was the beginning of it. I ran to the top of the escalator as fast as I could and looked east, out toward Church Street at the Millenium hotel. The windows of the hotel are like a mirror, and in the reflection I saw Tower Two coming down.

How do you describe the sound of a 110-story building coming down directly above you? It sounded like what it was: a deafening tidal wave of building material coming down on my head. It appeared to be falling on the street directly where I was headed.

I turned to run back into the building. It was the instinctual thing to do. You're thinking, If you stay outside, you're running into it. If you go inside, it might not land there. So I turned and ran into the building, down into the mall, and that's when it hit. I dove to the ground, screaming at the top of my lungs, "Oh, no! Oh, no! Jenny and Ben! Jenny and Ben!" It wasn't a very creative response, but it was the only thing I could say. I was gonna die.

The explosion was extreme, the noise impossible to describe. I started crying. It's hard for me to imagine now that when I was on the ground awaiting my doom, hearing that noise, thousands of people were dying. That noise is a noise thousands of people heard when they died.

When it hit, everything went instantly black. You know how a little kid packs a pail of sand at the beach? That's what it was like in my mouth, my nose, my ears, my eyes, everything packed with debris. I spat it out. I puked, mostly out of horror. I felt myself: Am I intact? Can I move? I was all there. There was moaning. People were hurt and crying all around me.

Then I had my second reckoning with death. I'm alive, yeah. But I'm trapped beneath whatever fell on top of me and this place is filled with smoke and dust. This is how I'm gonna die—and this was worse. Because I was going to be cognizant of my death. I was going to be trapped in a hole and it was going to fill with smoke and they were going to find me like one of those guys buried in Pompeii.

I sat there thinking of my wife and son again. It wasn't like seeing the photos of Jenny and Ben that I had on my desk, though. The images I had were of them without me. Images of knowing that I'd never touch them again. As I sat there, thinking of them, I suddenly got this presence of mind: I gotta try to survive.

I tore off my shirt and wrapped it around my mouth and nose to keep some of the smoke out. I started crawling. It was absolutely pitch-black. I had no idea where I was crawling to, but I had to keep trying. It's haunting to think about it now.

I saw a light go on. I can't say I was happy, because I was horrified, but that light was hope.

Luckily, I was buried with a fireman. I got over to him and stuck to this guy like a sticky burr on a bear's ass. He was frazzled, but he had it a lot more together than I did. I was, like, "What are we gonna do?" You can't imagine the ability to have rational thought at that point. I was purely in survival mode. It wasn't like, The smoke is traveling this way, so I'll go that way to the fresh air. It's whatever presents itself.

The fireman looked like a big Irish guy. Big, bushy mustache. He had an axe. He was looking at a wall, and it looked solid, but when he wiped his hand on it, it was glass, a glass wall looking into a Borders bookstore. There was a door right next to it. He smashed the door and it spread open.

Everyone gravitated to the light. Now there was a bunch of us. People were screaming. We got into Borders, went upstairs, and got through the doors heading outside. The dust was so thick, there was barely any light.

At this point, I still had no idea what was going on. I didn't know if we were being bombed or what. I didn't know if this was over or if it was just beginning.

I took off into the cloud. I crossed Church Street, and some light started coming in, and I could see a little bit. I saw a woman standing there, horrified, crying, lost. I stopped and said, "Are you okay? Are you okay?" She couldn't speak. I kept going.

I went along Vesey Street, using it as a guide. It started clearing up more and more, and I got to an intersection that was completely empty. That's where I saw one of the weirdest things—a cameraman near a van with the NBC peacock on it, doubled over with his camera, crying.

I was all disoriented. I saw a turned-over bagel cart, and I grabbed a couple of Snapples. I used one to rinse out my mouth and wash my face. I drank some of the other. Then I started running again. It was chaos.

Even though I'd been around these streets a million times, I was completely lost. I looked up and saw my building, 1 World Trade Center, in flames. I looked for the other tower because I always use the two buildings as my North Star. I couldn't see it. I stood there thinking, It doesn't make sense. At that angle, it was apparent how devastating it all was. I looked up and said, "Hundreds of people died today." I was trying to come to terms with it—to intellectualize it. My wife's family is Jewish, and her grandparents talk about the Holocaust and the ability of humans to be cruel and kill one another. This is a part of a pattern of human behavior, I told myself. And I just happen to be very close to this one.

Maybe it seems an odd reaction in hindsight. But I was just trying to grab on to something, some sort of logic or justification, rather than let it all overwhelm me. I was raised Irish-Catholic, and I consider myself a spiritual person. I did thank God for getting me out of there for my kid. But I also tend to be a pretty logical thinker. I'm alive because I managed to find a space that had enough support structure that it didn't collapse on me. I'm alive because the psycho in the plane decided to hit at this angle as opposed to that angle. I'm alive because I went down this stairwell instead of that stairwell. I can say that now. But at that moment, I was just trying to give myself some sanity.

I was still running when I heard another huge sound. I didn't know it at the time, but it was the other tower—my tower—coming down. A cop on the street saw me and said, "Buddy, are you okay?" It was obvious that he was spooked by looking at me. Aside from being caked with dust, I had blood all over me that wasn't mine. He was trying to help, but I could tell he was shocked by what he was seeing.

I was looking for a pay phone to call my wife, but every one I passed was packed. My wife never entertained for a minute

I started running toward where my brother Chris worked at NYU. I'm the last of six in my family. The two oldest are girls, the four youngest, boys. Chris is the second oldest above me. The classic older brother. The one who'd put you down and give you noogies. He probably would have had the best view of the whole thing going on. But he'd left his office, thinking, My brother is dead. He walked home to Brooklyn across the Manhattan Bridge, unable to look back.

On my way to NYU, I met this guy— a stranger named Gary—who had a cell phone. He tried and tried and couldn't get through to Boston. I said, "I gotta get to NYU," and left him. But he kept calling Boston and eventually got through to my family. At that point, four of my five siblings were at the house. My wife's father was on his way from New York with a black suit in the car.

The people at NYU took me in. They were great. I said, "I don't need anything. Just call my family." They kept on trying to get through. They couldn't, they couldn't. Finally, they got through.

I said, "Jenny, it's me." And there was a moan. It was this voice I'd never heard before in my life. And I was saying, "I'm alive. I'm alive. I love you. I love you. I love you." We cried and cried. Then the phone went dead.

At that point, I went into the bathroom to clean myself off, and suddenly I couldn't open my eyes anymore. They were swollen. I knew I wasn't blind, but if

that I could be alive. She had turned on the TV and said, "Eighty-first floor. Both buildings collapsed. There's not a prayer." It was difficult for her to look at Ben because she was having all these feelings. "Should I be grateful that I have him? Is he going to be a reminder of Mike every time I look at him?" At the time, these thoughts just go through your head.

Finally, I got to a pay phone where there was a woman just kind of looking up. I shoved her out of the way. I guess it was kind of harsh, but I had to get in touch with my family. I dialed Boston and a recording said, "Six dollars and twenty-five cents, please." So I pulled out a quarter and called my brother at NYU. I got his voice mail. "I'm alive! I'm alive! Call Jenny! Let everyone know I'm alive!" It was 10:34.

I opened my eyes toward any amount of light there was intense, intense pain. I didn't feel this while I was running. It seemed to happen as soon as I was safe and the adrenaline came out of me.

At the NYU health center, the doctors said, "Yeah, your eyes are scratched to shit." They put drops in them, but they needed more sophisticated equipment to see what was going on. I wound up having 147 fiberglass splinters taken out of my eyes.

Chris came back from Brooklyn to pick me up, and I held on to him and hugged him. Later, he said, "You know, Michael, this is why I stuffed you in sleeping bags and beat on you all those years as a kid. Just to toughen you up for something like this."

When we got back to my place, I collapsed and it all hit me. I cried like I've never cried in my life. I finally let loose, and it felt better. My brother helped me pack, and we got to Westchester, where my wife and family had gone. Jenny came running to the door. I can remember hearing the dum, dum, dum, dum, dum of her footsteps.

My mother was there. My dad. My father-in-law. They all hugged me. Then they gave me my son. I could tell by the noises he was making that he was happy. I hugged him and sort of started the healing process there.

Later, I went to Maine to sit by the ocean for a few days and get my head together. I saw all of my old friends. It was amazing. Everyone I know in my life has called me to tell me they love me. It's like having your funeral without having to die.

For a while right after, I wondered, How the hell am I going to work again? How am I going to give a damn about selling someone a T-1 line? I had a list of people who were going to be my business for the next year, hundreds of people, all on my desk—blown up. For the life of me, I can't dredge up those names. That will cost me a quarter of my income, maybe more. You know what? Who cares? I'm alive and I'm here. A big deal has gone to big deal.

I lost a friend in 2 World Trade Center. He was one of those guys you liked as soon as you met him. Howard Boulton. Beautiful person. His baby was born three months ahead of mine. He was on the eighty-fourth floor and I was on the eighty-first. The last conversation he had with his wife was by telephone. He told her, "Something happened to 1 World Trade Center. It's very bad. I don't think Michael Wright is okay. I'm coming home." I like to think Howard wasn't scared like I wasn't scared in the stairwell. I like to think that he heard a rumble like I heard a rumble and then he was gone.

I went to his funeral. To see his wife and his baby—it would have made you sad even if you didn't know him. But it was much more loaded for me. Here was a perfect reflection of what could've been.

I don't wonder, Why me? Some people say, "You made it out; you're destined for great things." Great, I tell them. I made it out, now why not put a little pressure on me while you're at it. ▮

"A Day of Terror: A Critic's Notebook; Live Images Make Viewers Witnesses to Horror" [EXCERPT]

by Caryn James, THE NEW YORK TIMES, September 12, 2001

From the time the second plane crashed flaming through the World Trade Center on live television yesterday, viewers became horrified eyewitnesses to terrorist attacks in progress, a phenomenal sight that separates the political violence of our television era from all others.

Though the attack was quickly and frequently compared to the Japanese attack on Pearl Harbor, Americans experienced this assault in a far different way, watching disasters accumulate faster than they could be absorbed emotionally. Many commentators echoed Franklin D. Roosevelt's response to Pearl Harbor. Dan Rather said, "This is another day that no doubt will live in infamy." But no resonant phrase emerged to define yesterday's tragedy the way Roosevelt's radio-age words defined the World War II attack. In this visual era, the incredible live images, replayed throughout the day until their reality sunk in, defined the events. As Senator Charles E. Schumer, Democrat of New York, said on camera, "This is Pearl Harbor, 21st century."

. . . The images were terrifying to watch, yet the coverage was strangely reassuring simply because it existed with such imme-

diacy, even when detailed information was scarce. Imagine how much worse the nightmare would have been if broadcasting had been destroyed. On a day of death, television was a lifeline to what was happening.

. . . The least comforting moments involved the president. Mr. Bush first appeared briefly, at 9:30 A.M., surrounded by Florida schoolchildren to whom he had been reading when he learned of the attack. And even though he announced that the country had suffered "an apparent ter-

rorist attack," that live appearance was more reassuring than the taped statement later from an air force base in Louisiana. The audio was not working when some networks first played that tape, creating an ominous sense that things were not under control as much as he said. Through the day, some of the most harrowing reports told viewers what they did not know: where the president was. The unseen image of Mr. Bush meeting with advisers "in a bunker," as reporters said, was al-most as chilling as the violence on screen.

When he spoke to the nation at 8:30 last night, Mr. Bush had a typically stiff, teleprompted delivery in a speech that, contrasting the "shattered steel" of the buildings with the "steel of American re-solve," strained for phrasemaking it could not achieve. "Today our nation saw evil" was the only memorable phrase. But what mattered was that he was visible, live from the Oval Office, offering a sense of stability and a sense of a future. . . . ▌▌

"Americans Tune In and Stress Out" [EXCERPT]

by Howard Kurtz, THE WASHINGTON POST, September 20, 2001

Nearly three-quarters of Americans say they have felt depressed over last week's terrorist attacks, nearly half have had difficulty concentrating, and one-third are having trouble sleeping, according to a survey released yesterday.

While huge majorities are glued to the coverage of what the pundits call "America's new war"—and give the media stunningly high marks—three-quarters say it's scary to watch and nearly two-thirds say they're addicted to the news.

"Americans are more saddened, more frightened, and more fatigued by what they are watching than was the case during the Gulf War," says the report by the Pew Research Center.

. . . . The round-the-clock coverage of the attacks on New York and Washington, with its pictures of death and destruction and constant talk of a grueling war to come, is exacting a heavy psychological toll. Women, parents, and urban residents are the hardest hit, says the survey of 1,200 adults questioned September 13 to 17.

Seventy-nine percent of women say they have felt depressed over the recent events, compared with 62 percent of men. More women also say they have trouble sleeping.

More parents (76 percent) than non-parents (69 percent) say they have felt depressed. And perhaps because they feel more vulnerable, 77 percent of those in major East and West Coast cities report feeling depressed, compared with 69 percent of those elsewhere.

There is a spiritual response as well: Sixty-nine percent say they are praying more. And 30 percent of parents say they are trying to restrict how much of the coverage their children watch.

But few, for the moment, are blaming journalists.

"The coverage is providing a prism on exactly what has happened," said Andrew Kohut, the center's director. "I don't think it's a case of people being frightened by the spin put on it or the way it's portrayed. This is such a devastating event."

It is a compelling one as well. Eighty-one percent say they are keeping a television or radio on for updates, while 46 percent say they are reading the newspaper more closely. . . . The Internet is also having an impact; a third of those surveyed say they go online for the latest news. . . . ▌

BYRON PITTS | *Correspondent, CBS News:*

MY COLLEAGUE, MIKA BRZEZINSKI, and I ran inside Public School 89 to escape the collapsing towers. It was the first open door we came across as smoke, ash, and fire chased us up the West Side Highway. As we ran in the back door, teachers were calmly evacuating schoolchildren out the front door. Mika and I found a phone in what looked like a storage room. We stood near each other in silence as a black cloud passed by, blocking out the sunlight. In an instant, day had turned to dusk.

Mika, who had lost her shoes and was standing in her stocking feet, phoned in the first report, while I ventured outside to check on the situation. We both looked like hell. But we were alive.

When I first stepped out from the elementary school, I couldn't breathe and I couldn't make sense of what I was seeing. It looked like it was snowing. Everything was light gray—the street, the sidewalk, and the cars, even the few people walking around. I ran back in to take a deep breath and to process what I had just seen. I peeked in on Mika, told her things looked relatively safe and that I'd be back in a few minutes.

But as I turned to leave, I bumped chest first into a fireman. He was covered from head to toe in a thick layer of ash. I offered him water that Mika had found in the storage room. He accepted it, walked in, and took off his helmet.

There was a pile of clothes in the room—a collection of children's winter garments, perhaps for a charity of some sort. This seemed like as good a cause as any, so we grabbed a child's sweater and wiped off the fireman's face. He thanked us.

I asked him if he would mind being interviewed live via telephone for CBS News. He didn't answer so I took that as a yes, or at least not a no.

Once on the air, I asked the fireman what had happened and what he had seen. "I lost all my men. When the building came down, I got separated from my men," he said.

"How many men?" I asked.

"At least ten," he said, "and there are hundreds more missing." He asked us to call his wife to let her know that he was okay.

I asked him if there was anything he would like to say to his wife in case she's listening. "Tell her I love her. I'm okay, but I must go back and find my men."

At that moment, I noticed that the fireman was crying. He wiped his eyes with the child's sweater and then walked out the door into the darkness.

"The Inner Strengths of a Vulnerable City"

by Kurt Andersen, TIME, September 24, 2001

During my long walk home Tuesday, it was on a block of lower Third Avenue—that is, the Bowery—that I first felt reassured. All the storefront missions were hopping, their doors wide open. The mission workers were on the sidewalk exuding matter-of-fact competence as they offered their services—water, bathrooms, food, telephones, first aid—to the thousands of anxious strangers passing by. A few of the regular clientele, people accustomed to walking the streets dazed and dirty, stood aside, watching their temporarily down-and-out fellow citizens accept handouts.

New Yorkers are known for being jaded, and they are, but the iconic toughness is also a pose. It isn't just a matter of 8 million cynics who turn out to be romantics when you scratch them. As a practical matter, liv-

ing here requires some willed sangfroid because living here also requires, more than anywhere else in America, an exhausting everyday vulnerability. We travel on subways packed shoulder to shoulder with exotic strangers close enough to smell their hair, and in taxis we put our lives in the hands of other random strangers who may or may not speak our language or know where they're going. We walk down sidewalks insanely dense with people and data, sidestepping peddlers, beggars, dog turds, and gaping steel holes that descend into basement caverns. We live in a teeming throng, exposed. And we like it that way. Because life in the open has two sides: We make ourselves vulnerable to ugliness and annoyance and danger because that's the price of remaining vulnerable to serendipity and beauty and even the odd epiphany.

We come here and stay, as E. B. White wrote of New Yorkers after the last World War, because we're "willing to be lucky." We're game. And lately in this city, as crime has plummeted and Wall Street has flourished, it has been easy to forget that luck,

like vulnerability, has a flip side. A willingness to be lucky implies a willingness to be unlucky. As a result of the reduction in the city's homicide rate, more than 5,000 lives have been saved over the past eight years. And now: 5,000 murders in one day.

In fact, White's willingness to be lucky—by which he meant pluck and hustle—is the American predisposition. Everyone (including us New Yorkers) tends to think of this place as radically unlike the rest of America. But now we know differently. Wide-open, vulnerable New York was targeted with such staggering precision and viciousness because the city, more than any other, actually does live up to the demonic Taliban caricature. We are the bin Ladenites' worst nightmare. We are rich.

We swagger. We enjoy ourselves. From Wall Street to the media conglomerates of Midtown to the vast immigrant neighborhoods in all the boroughs, we embody the power and the glory of globalization. We are a profoundly secular city; nowhere else in America are people freer to worship their own gods or to be godless. No place outside Israel has more Jews. Blasphemy is common, irreverence is obligatory. Art is at least as important as religion. Eccentric ideas and profane entertainment flourish. Women do just as they please.

In other words, the terrorists attacked us for precisely the reasons we choose to live here. And, we can only hope after all this, choose to stay—still willing to be lucky. ∎

"Smoke and Stench Cannot Mask the Strength to Rebuild" [EXCERPT]

by Pete Hamill, DAILY NEWS, September 13, 2001

On the morning after, a dirty yellowish cloud rose from the mutilated stumps of the twin towers. It drifted east over City Hall Park and then picked up a wind and moved more quickly up Broadway. Its fine ash fell on the masked policemen, on a few lone pedestrians, on the FBI agents and on the National Guardsman in combat gear, who sat high on a Humvee at the corner of Walker Street. The air smelled like scorched paint.

All the shops were closed below Canal Street, except for the Korean deli at Leonard Street, which had stayed open feeding hungry locals and cops. Now there was no bread left, no bagels—only coffee and cakes. The rituals of morning were disrupted. Even the newspapers belonged to some northern part of the city, above Houston Street, above 14th Street. Down here, people lived for a second day under the dirty yellow cloud of fanaticism. . . .

The night before, power failed from Worth Street to beyond the World Trade Center. The streets that night were eerie, as if hurled by the explosion back into the 19th century, when so many of the buildings were erected.

All of Church Street was packed with 16-wheelers (I counted 14 of them), all pointed downtown, waiting to haul away the wreckage. Plows, backhoes, generator trucks were on their flanks. The lights cast long, unsteady shadows, filled with spectres.

At a little before 11, I saw three exhausted firemen cross Chambers Street, walking north, their faces etched with a failure that was not a failure of the heart. Behind them, under mounds of steel, glass, plaster, carpeting, desks, beams, and girders, lay more than 200 of their comrades. Men crushed by the acts of lunatics, men who died trying to save human life. Looks said more than words. The ash-smeared coats of these survivors wore their names: Healey, Moriarty, Heaney. The indomitable Irishry, as Yeats once said. But it seemed obscene to stop and ask them how they felt. The look in their eyes said more than any words.

Now, in the daylight, we looked down Church Street from Reade Street and just past the post office, saw the black spiky shards of the facade of the north tower. They filled a space in front of the Borders bookstore that had been empty 24 hours

earlier, so they must have blown outwards in the horrific collapse of the tower. Smoke rose from the mound of rubble behind them and a giant crane hovered above the ruins, as if urging itself, above all, to do no harm. Two birds, tough New York pigeons, suddenly flew past St. Peter's on Barclay Street, made a circle to the west in the grainy air, then raced back east.

A block away was West Broadway, with police cars from Duxbury, Mass., Whitpain, Mass., and Suffolk County parked at the curbs, and the men who drove them down among the rescuers. In the tiny triangular park where Hudson Street meets West Broadway, the leaves of the shrubs were coated with dusty ash, the streets were white, the sidewalk covered with a litter of exploded rental agreements, memos, jottings on memo paper. Soldiers in camouflage uniforms controlled crowds and traffic. In the distance, firemen on ladders poured water into the smoldering rubble. Above them was the smoky open space where the twin towers used to be.

On Greenwich Street, the Salvation Army Emergency and Disaster Unit offered coffee and water to rescuers. Now immense dump trucks, loaded with ripped, twisted metal, turned into Chambers Street, heading west, and on to a dump at 59th Street. One held a mashed red car, and a fireman poured water into it to be sure it held no fire. The water hissed against crumpled metal. This is what London must have been like on mornings during the Blitz. . . .

From the bridge over the highway that leads to Stuyvesant High School, the view was filled with the evidence of invincible New York will. Downtown, among the cops, and firemen, and National Guardsmen, hundreds of trade unionists—ironworkers, welders, carpenters— were walking toward the ruins; big, tough men, ready to cut steel. They wore hardhats and orange vests. They carried the tools of their glorious trades, those trades that built this city with brains, and muscle, and craft. The men of the trade unions. They would try this morning to save the living. The building could come later.

Uptown from the Stuyvesant Bridge, there were trucks from Mazzochi Demolition, and trucks carrying huge portable lights, and backloaders, and police trucks: all waiting their call. Waiting to go to the ruins, to claw and pull at bent steel and then to haul it away. The trucks were all the way up the West Side Highway, as far as eyes could see.

The men who drove and manned those trucks knew that ahead of them, in the dark voids of the destroyed twin towers, human beings might still be alive. Might be hoping for one more day, one more hour, one more chance at living, at hugging the people they loved, at romping with kids and grandchildren, slaying time at ballgames and beaches. If those trapped

men and women could only see this New York army at work, they would be filled with the adrenaline of hope.

In the lobby of Stuyvesant High School, cots awaited the casualties. Doctors and nurses waited to ease pain and save human life. Medicine, bandages, and unguents were ready. There was food here, and drink, and hearts much bigger than those doomed towers. But while I was there, not a single living casualty arrived.

And from the ruins, that yellow cloud, made of pain and death and religious zealotry, created by twisted minds and hardened hearts, kept rising over the city. The stench of it poisoned the air. Sirens wailed their terrible song. But that sinister cloud would not prevail. The world's God-sick party of death would not win. There on the ground, on the day after our worst calamity, were the toughest people anywhere on Earth. They would remove that smoke from our sky. And when it was gone, they would work, as they always do, for life itself. They would drink. They would sing. They would dance. ▐

"In Charge"

by Elizabeth Kolbert, THE NEW YORKER, September 24, 2001

Shortly before nine o'clock on Tuesday morning last week, Mayor Rudolph Giuliani was on Fifth Avenue, at Fiftieth Street, on his way to City Hall, when he got word that a plane had crashed into the north tower of the World Trade Center. He sped downtown and got there in time to witness what he subsequently described as "the most horrific scene I've ever seen in my whole life." The Mayor spoke to some of the fire commanders at the scene, including the chief of the department, Peter Ganci, who was killed moments later. In a gruesome irony, the city's new emergency command center was situated directly inside the World Trade Center—not in one of the two towers that were hit but in a third building, which also lay in ruins by

the end of the day. Since that location was obviously unsafe, Giuliani went to a suite of city offices a block away, at 75 Barclay Street, where he and his aides intended to set up an alternative command post. When the first World Trade Center tower collapsed, debris started to rain down from the ceiling of 75 Barclay, and they had to evacuate that building as well. They had just finished an impromptu news conference at Chambers Street and West Broadway, and had begun walking north, when the second tower collapsed. It was at that point that the Mayor of the city of New York, along with everybody else in lower Manhattan, found himself running for his life.

Mayors always rush to the scene of disasters; this is as much a part of the job as submitting budgets and making sure the garbage gets picked up on time. No mayor, however, has ever had to react to a disaster of the magnitude of last week's, and few could have done so with more forcefulness, or steadiness of purpose, than Giuliani. On the day of the attack, the Mayor spoke publicly at least half a dozen times, the last around midnight, and then he went back to the scene to speak to the rescue teams working through the night. Each time he spoke, he managed to convey at once grief and resolve, and his presence offered the kind of reassurance so disconcertingly absent in Washington, where the President was, for much of the day, missing.

"New York is still here," the Mayor said at one point. "We've undergone tremendous losses, and we're going to grieve for them horribly, but New York is going to be here tomorrow morning, and it's going to be here forever." He described speaking to Ganci, who had been a member of the Fire Department for thirty-three years, just before he died, and telling him, "God bless you." And he urged the people of the city to try to resume their normal lives without bitterness.

"Hatred, prejudice, and anger are what caused this terrible tragedy, and the people of the city of New York should act differently," he said. "We should act bravely. We should act in a tolerant way. We should go about our business, and we should show these people that they can't stop us." By all accounts, the command center the Mayor eventually did establish, at a location that reporters were asked not to divulge, functioned effectively. "It was magnificent, really," Representative Jerrold Nadler, a frequent critic of the Mayor, said after attending a meeting there.

Andrew Kirtzman, a political reporter for NY1, the city's cable news channel, was running alongside Giuliani on the morning of the tragedy. Kirtzman described the Mayor as entirely composed, even though, for nearly an hour, no one seemed to know where he should go. At one point, Kirtzman recalled, the Mayor bumped into a young black police officer: She said something to him, and, like a father, he touched her on the cheek. Even-

tually, he found a temporary office in a fire station, but since all the crews at the station had already left for the World Trade Center, someone had to jimmy the lock in order to let him in.

One of the mysteries of Giuliani's tenure has always been why, in moments of civic calm, he creates such havoc, and then, in genuine crises, behaves so calmly. This mystery will never entirely be solved; the attack occurred on the very day that the city's mayoral primary was to have taken place—it was postponed until September 25th—and there are now fewer than four months left in his term. But the role that the Mayor played last week was one that he, at least, had apparently fore-seen for himself. Giuliani had pushed for the construction of the new emergency command center, widely derided at the time as his "bunker," and, even though he made a dreadful miscalculation in putting it inside the World Trade Center, his concerns about New York's vulnerability, and the need for sure leadership in case the worst occurred, were more than borne out. Too much of the past year had been given over to the Mayor's usual battles— with his estranged wife, with the city comptroller, with museums that he accused of offending decency. Now, in the context of last week's terrible events, something of Giuliani has been restored to him and, by extension, to the city. ▮

"Liberties: A Grave Silence" [EXCERPT]

by Maureen Dowd, THE NEW YORK TIMES, September 12, 2001

. . . For many hours, the most eerie thing about the American capital, under attack for the first time since the British burned the White House in the War of 1812, was the stillness at the center of the city. New York was a clamorous inferno of pain, confusion, and fear, with Mayor Rudolph Giuliani on the scene in the rubble of the World Trade Center towers and on TV trying to reassure residents about schools and transportation and hospitals.

Manhattan had the noise of the grave. Washington had the silence of the grave. Downtown you could smell the smoke

and see the plume rising from a Pentagon full of carnage and fire and see the flag over the emptied White House flying at half-staff.

But until the nation's leaders reappeared on television after nightfall to speak of what President Bush called their "quiet, unyielding anger," no one understood what had happened. No one knew what might happen next. Would there be a gas attack? Would the White House blow up? Would another plane crash into the Capitol?

People were so hungry for clues that they gathered, as their parents did after Pearl Harbor, around radios, huddled in small groups a block from a cordoned-off White House....

On a gorgeous blue fall day, terrorism had turned into war. The city that leads the world took on a weird neutron-bomb quality. No one even tried to pretend, as we are supposed to, that no matter what, terrorists cannot disrupt our government.

For much of the day we weren't sure where the president was. There were statements floating in from him from various secure zones in the air or underground. The vice president was out of sight. We didn't know where the first lady was. The secretary of state was in the air somewhere. The Capitol had been evacuated. Congressional leaders had gone off to a bunker somewhere. The Joint Chiefs of Staff could not be immediately accounted for.

The CIA and FBI were stunned. Most vividly at his post was [Secretary of Defense] Donald Rumsfeld, who helped rescue victims at the Pentagon and stayed all day in the smoky command center.

White House officials had fled the building five minutes after the plane crashed into the Pentagon at 9:45 A.M., streaming out with some men screaming and some women barefoot and carrying their high heels....

Federal buildings were evacuated, coffee shops shuttered, dress shops barred. A few tourists wandered around in shorts looking confused as military planes patrolled above. D.C. police carried rifles, and Secret Service agents in black Mustangs and green Luminas blocked off the streets adjacent to the White House.... ▌▌

SCOTT PELLEY | *Correspondent, CBS News:*

AT GROUND ZERO, as the area around the sight of the World Trade Center disaster came to be known, firemen dug with their hands, searching for any sign of life. There were one and a half million tons of ruins and nearly 3,000 people inside. "It's just incredible, indescribable," an exhausted fireman told me. "We are standing on the roof of the building and as we're digging out, all you see is the tops of fire engines and cars, there's stuff and people everywhere."

"Everybody's working together," another fireman said, "piece by piece, hand by hand. The whole city is trying to get people out."

Volunteers marched in off the street, including retired firemen, ironworkers, nurses, and tourists. They set up bucket brigades to move the wreckage, hand over hand, a few pounds at a time. In the first hours, I saw a great deal of hope. Rescuers climbed the mountain of debris expecting miracles. Fred Clark, a carpenter who helped build the World Trade Center in 1969, was back to take it apart. "What I see now is heartbreaking, but I'm hopeful," he told me. "I'm here to find somebody still alive."

There was one miracle. Nearly a day after the attack, John McLoughlin, a Port Authority police officer, was pulled out alive. "I was here when they pulled out the police officer," Dr. Tony Dajer, of New York University Hospital, told me. "He was in very good shape actually." But Officer McLoughlin would be the last amazing story of survival.

Ambulances rushed in, but did not rush out. Dr. Lincoln Cleveland, also with New York University Hospital, stood amid the devastation with no one to save. "You can read a couple of things into that," he told me. "Either people are buried and they're going to start bringing bodies out, or just everybody died." No one was found after the first twenty-four hours.

But for me, what I'll never forget is the faces of the lost that looked out from photographs plastered onto parked cars, lampposts, and mailboxes throughout the city. Families posted thousands of missing-persons fliers. One man walked up to me holding up the picture of his best friend in the hope that a passerby might recognize the face. "He has a two-and-a-half-year-old daughter. He's the godfather of my children," he said. "Have you seen him in there?" For the most part, the pleas of these families would never be answered.

"New York Dispatch: Family Room"

by David Grann, THE NEW REPUBLIC, October 1, 2001

On the fourth day I went to get a sense of the devastation. The street outside my building in lower Manhattan was still cordoned off on either end by police, and you needed an escort and proof of ID to get in or out. The young officer who stood guard on the corner said that two of his colleagues from the police station next door were missing. "A man and a woman," he said. "We're still hoping."

I headed uptown to the Pierre Hotel, where I heard that the families from Cantor Fitzgerald—a bond-trading firm that had lost some 700 of its 1,000 New York employees in the World Trade Center attack—had set up an emergency center. It was in the Grand Ballroom on the second floor, where weddings and executive banquets were normally held, a place that seemed utterly incongruous for a crisis room. It was opened, along with the hotel, in 1930 and, according to the hotel's brochures, had "received royalty, world leaders, and celebrities." Outside the main door, the company had set up tables with information packets, including hot lines for "investigative tips," "hospitals," and "police." There was a place to fill out missing-person reports, and a few people gathered around it. The forms were eight pages thick and asked for anything that might identify the missing, including dental records ("partial plate," "braces,"

"no teeth") and objects in the body ("pacemaker," "bullets," "steel plate"). On page four there was a checklist for build, race, and hair color, as well as items like wigs, toupees, and transplants. "Facial Hair Style: ___Fu Manchu ___Whiskers Under Lower Lip ___ Mutton Chops ___ Pencil Thin Upper Lip ___N/Applicable." There was also a checklist for dominant hand, fingernail type ("natural," "artificial"), nail characteristics ("dirty," "misshapen," "decorated," "tobacco stain"), complexion, dress, and, on the second to last page, a "DNA Donor Information" form.

Inside the ballroom, tacked along the back walls, were sheaths of white paper, each with a picture and details of one of the missing. Some were written by hand, as if in haste, others typed in bold computer fonts. One said, "Adriane Scibetta 5 feet w/brown hair/brown eyes," and had a photo of her with three little girls. Another said, "Francis (also goes by Frank or Fran) 28 years old/5'10"-170 lbs. Light brown hair cut very short. Green eyes . . . two tattoos: a Shamrock in Irish flag colors with the word 'Mom' written in the middle of his right upper arm. Also a tattoo of the Chinese symbol for Mother on his right arm." Underneath was a picture of him, his sleeve rolled up, so that you could see the word "Mom" etched on his right bicep. Next to him was a picture of

Amy O'Doherty. It had been mimeo-
graphed and her face was faded. Underneath it listed three "distinguishing
characteristics":

Freckles

Large Chest

Diamond stud earring

I walked from one wall to the next,
staring at the faces, reading the captions
above them: "Have you seen Mr. Hash-
mukhrai Parmar?"…"Have you seen these
two cousins?"

A woman with two boys was putting
up a picture, this one mounted on construction paper so it would stand out.
"Put it up over here," the woman said to
one of the boys. "There's more space."

As you stepped deeper into the room
there were dozens of round tables draped
with white cloths and surrounded with
gold-painted chairs. Four to eight people
were sitting around each, lit by rococo
chandeliers. Off to the side was a buffet
table with Cokes and Perrier in buckets of
ice, and ham and cheese sandwiches on
French bread, neatly sliced, with mustard
and lettuce. Waiters moved through the
room holding silver platters, as if it were
just another company Christmas party.
But as I looked more closely I noticed a
number on each of the tables, beginning
with 101 and going up to 106, and I realized that these were the floor numbers
where the missing had worked—that the
room had been arranged according to
where the victims had, in all likelihood,
last been seen. There was a steady hum as

people leaned over the tables, exchanging
information and working their cell
phones.

At one point, as I was standing there, a
woman ran up to me and said excitedly,
"Are you Martin?"

"No," I said, not sure if Martin was
one of the missing or someone who po-
tentially had information. "I'm sorry."

When I said that I was a reporter a
man nearby asked if I had been to ground
zero recently. His brother, he said, was
missing. "First our tactic was to find anyone who saw him," he explained. "Now
our tactic is to find anyone who made it
out of these top floors."

He drew a diagram on a piece of paper,
showing me where all the stairwells and
exit routes were and how the forces had
brought down the building. "My brother
is strong," he said. "He may have made it
into the basement."

Eventually I sat down at one of the tables, marked 101. An elderly couple,
Carlton and Coletta Valvo, had just arrived from California. Because the airports were originally closed, they had
driven to Vancouver and flown to Toronto
and then rented a car and rode all night to
New York. The father had graying hair
and thick black glasses that made his eyes
look enormous. He said his son, Carlton
Jr., was thirty-eight years old and a vice
president. He had just gone to work for
Cantor Fitzgerald and had a wife and a
seven-year-old daughter. "He spoke to my
other son on his cell phone and said, 'I

don't know if we can survive. There's smoke. I got to go.' "

"You could hear screaming," said the mother, Coletta. "Then the phone went dead."

"I'm a doctor," the father continued. "I have a sense of reality, but—"

"We still have hope," his wife interjected. "There are miracles."

Later, while I was talking to someone else, Dr. Valvo tapped my shoulder and said he wanted to show me something. He took my arm and led me to the back, where hundreds of photos were pasted. "There," he said, pointing. "By the American flag."

Amid the many photos, I saw a young face staring out with the same Coke-bottle glasses as his father. "We gave him that Hawaiian shirt at his brother's wedding party," he said.

When we sat back down the others were talking about ways their family members might have escaped. One man who had been at the table earlier, we were informed, had said that his brother was a Navy Seal and could spend at least six days in the rubble without food or water. Mrs. Valvo said that there was a gap between when her son had called and when the building collapsed, leaving the family some hope that he had survived.

But Dr. Valvo didn't seem so sure, and when the others weren't listening, he showed me a copy of a leaflet from the American Red Cross he had gotten for his daughter-in-law and seven-year-old grandchild. "I thought it might help." It said, "after the disaster . . . The following common, normal reactions may be experienced: Disorientation . . . difficulty concentrating . . . trouble sleeping . . . headaches . . . skin disorders . . . sadness/apathy . . . guilt/self-blame . . . moodiness/irritability/emotional outbursts . . . increased use of caffeine, alcohol, or drugs . . . 'flashbacks' . . . nausea . . . changes in sexual desire or functioning."

On the back of the leaflet it had a special section on how to help the young who had lost family members. "If they are upset about what has happened, children may experience the same reactions as adults, plus the following: Bedwetting, thumb sucking, or other earlier-age behaviors . . ."

There was a podium up front and a man rose to address the crowd. He said that he worked for Cantor Fitzgerald and asked everyone to fill out missing-person reports. "If you haven't done that yet, please immediately go to the reception area. . . . Are there any questions?"

A slight woman got up and asked if rescue workers had found anyone from the company's floors yet. He said there had been "rumors" but nobody so far. (A woman later told me that she had seen a man crying yesterday into his cell phone after hearing that his relative was alive—but that the man was now back in the room with everyone else. "I guess it wasn't true," she said.)

Not long after, a gentleman stood from table 105. "What were the evacuation procedures for our floor?" The man at the podium said he wasn't sure, when a woman leaped to her feet and said, "I don't understand what we're all doing here. There are a thousand employees missing and we are the only company that can't find anybody—not a single person—and we're sitting around eating sandwiches. Why aren't we doing something to get our people out of the basement who are stuck . . . under 70 feet of concrete?"

The man at the podium tried to speak but the woman cut him off: "You're a million-dollar company. Why aren't you bringing in engineers from around the country?"

"I understand your frustration. But we are not an engineering company. We are a financial service company."

A grief counselor who had sat down beside me told me that most people in the room still didn't want to talk to him—that most believed, even after four days, that they would find their loved ones. "No one is prepared for tragedy," he said later, "but these are people who are not normally struck by it."

In the center of the room, several families had gathered around two televisions, watching the latest news. I noticed one girl who had been staring at it for hours.

She had olive skin and looked like she was in high school. She told me her twenty-nine-year-old brother was missing. "My mother keeps saying, 'Thank God I have you,'" she told me. "I think my mother is still in denial and my father knows but he won't speak. I think my mother and I are just blocking it out and my father is thinking about what my brother was going through, but I can't think about that because if I think about that . . . " On the television you could see the second tower collapsing. "I'm never going to be the same," she said. "I was just thinking of going into sales because I'm such a people person. . . . But I'm not going to be that person anymore. I just want to sit behind a desk and not speak to anyone."

On the television you could hear a tape recording from Kenneth Van Auken, a Cantor Fitzgerald employee who called his wife and said on their answering machine: "I love you. I'm in the World Trade Center. And the building was hit by something. I don't know if I'm going to get out. But I love you very much. I hope I'll see you later. Bye."

People seemed eager to talk to a reporter. They came up to me—in contrast with the grief counselors—and handed me posters, stuffing them in my hands and pockets. I filled notebook after notebook with their stories. At table 106, a thirty-four-year-old mother named Annette Vukosa leaned over and told me she had two children, a two-year-old and a seven-year-old. "The oldest doesn't want to hear his father might not come home," she said. "I told him, 'We're looking for your dad, but no matter what happens I really love you and I will take care of you.' But he said, 'My daddy's here. He's going to take care of me too.'" She paused. "When we used to go to Manhattan, his father would tell him, 'You see the tallest building? That's where I work.'"

I sat with her, looking at pictures of her family, until the room fell totally silent. Howard W. Lutnick, the head of the company, had arrived to give the latest updates on the search. He wore a black suit and his hair was slicked back over the top the way brokers often seem to prefer it. I had read in the papers that he was a fierce executive, someone who overwhelmed his rivals in the financial world. But as he surveyed the ballroom he seemed almost diminutive. He had survived Tuesday only because he had taken his son to school and had arrived at the twin towers just before they collapsed, as people were streaming out. "I'll do what I always do," he said now. "I'll tell you everything that I know. But I don't have all the answers and some of the things I say could be wrong and if it doesn't work out that way, I have just one rule: You can't be mad at me. Because I've had two people angry at me, as if somehow I did something." He paused, wiping his eyes. "So I just ask you, if someone is mad or angry or they think you did something wrong just try to remember . . . no one's better and no one's worse and no one's right and no one's

wrong. We're all suffering." He inhaled deeply. "So I'll tell you what I know. We've now confirmed that two of our employees' bodies have been found. Two people. They were on our floors. They did it with dental records. So for those of you who want me to, I'll say it as plain as I can: They are no longer looking for survivors. They are now in the process of trying to find our families. That's what they're doing."

The room filled with cries. I could see Dr. Valvo holding his wife, and the girl who had lost her brother slumped over, and Annette reaching for her sister. A moment later a young man rose in the center of the room and started to shout, "Don't you take our hope! Don't you take our hope!"

Lutnick said he wasn't trying to. But the man continued: "How can you tell us we won't find our families when they are still looking for them?"

"I'll tell you why," Lutnick said. "Because my brother Gary Lutnick called my sister that morning and said, 'I'm stuck on the 103rd floor. I am trapped and there is no way out.' "

He started to weep. "We are all on the same side," he said. "We all want our loved ones to be alive. We need them to be alive. They have to be alive. But you know what, they may not be. If you don't want that to be today, then I'm not telling you that it's today."

After a while Lutnick led everyone outside for a candlelight vigil and I broke off and headed home. As I came down Lexington Avenue I began to notice more and more white posters. They covered the railings, lampposts, and windows. It was getting dark but I could see the captions in the fading light: Chris M. Kirby . . . a carpenter . . . 152 lbs . . . blue eyes . . . William Kelly Jr. . . . 6 feet . . . 175 lbs . . . Timex Ironman watch on left wrist . . . Tonyell McDay . . . African American . . . approximately 5'4" . . . ruby ring on left pinky finger . . . Colleen Supinski . . . large blue eyes . . . long thick eye lashes . . . tiny wrists and fingers . . .

When I reached 27th Street the posters were everywhere, spilling out of newspaper boxes and telephone booths. I recognized some of the faces from the Pierre, but there were now hundreds more. I realized I had reached the Armory, where not just the people from Cantor Fitzgerald came, but all the victims' families filing their missing-person reports. Crowds of people were walking around, holding lit candles, and handing out posters. "Have you seen this person?" a man said, showing me a picture of a young woman. He held up a candle so I could see it better. I shook my head. But when he saw my reporter's pads, he started telling me about his daughter. I didn't have any more space in the notebooks, but I turned over a poster and, under the light of his candle, began to write. ∎

"Imagining the Hanson Family"

by Anna Quindlen, NEWSWEEK, September 24, 2001

As the wind began to shift northward and the ominous perfume of acrid smoke drifted down to the streets at the other end of the island, as the casualty lists grew longer and the stories of the missing less lined with hope, as the end of the world as we know it entered its postlude, it was the Hansons I fastened on. No telling why, exactly, except perhaps for the way their names appeared on the flight list, with that single number:

Peter Hanson, Massachusetts

Susan Hanson, Massachusetts

Christine Hanson, 2, Massachusetts

I could see them clear as the lambent blue sky that seemed to mock the mangled streets of lower Manhattan. I could see them in my imagination, the part of my mind that veered away from the footage of the flames and the endlessly falling. Maybe Christine, 2, had her own backpack to make her feel important going on the airplane. Maybe her parents carried a car seat to keep her safe on take-off and landing.

It seems as though each one of us had something that made us tremble: the airplane cell-phone call from husband to wife, saying he was going to take on the hijackers; the jaunty lament of the workers in the Twin Towers about the long climb down; the firefighters' helmets and boots found amid the rubble. "It was the people jumping out of the building holding hands," a woman whispered at daybreak, walking her dog.

For me it was the Hansons. I don't know why. It wasn't even that I knew much about them; I found out from news reports only that the three of them were going to visit family on the United flight from Boston to Los Angeles, the second plane to hit the World Trade Center. Instead I was struck by the idea of them, of what it feels like to be a mother, a father, to travel with your husband, your wife, with your 2-year-old daughter in the seat between you.

Despair was as thick in the air of the city as the smell of smoke. New Yorkers who often make eye contact only with the concrete beneath their feet walked, half dazed, glancing up at the sky that now seemed so dangerous. In the middle of the night a plane flew low and loud, and we started from our beds, seeing the familiar urban constellation of white lights out the window, looking for the bombs bursting in air.

Hope lies in the bright line that divides us from the men who did this thing: We can imagine the Hansons. The terrorists thought they were destroying buildings, monuments to capitalism and American military strength. But what they were doing was blowing families to bits. They left

behind, not so much a monumental mass of rubble, but tricycles, sweater drawers, love letters, flower beds, books, video cameras, unpaid bills, untidy kitchens, mothers, fathers, uncles, brothers, sons, daughters, friends, from Maine to California. And people have folded their hearts around all that messy detritus, so like their own, so that all the deaths have become a death in their family.

Anything can happen when human beings allow ideology to trump their humanity, when they elevate an idea above the lives of individuals. Anything can happen, and too often does. It becomes possible to bomb a black church and kill the four little girls inside. It becomes possible to execute a doctor who performs abortions, shoot him through the window of his own home while his children are nearby.

It becomes possible to drive a truck full of explosives into the side of the federal building in Oklahoma City and feel the ground buck beneath your feet, to turn a day-care center into a conflagration and refer to the babies and toddlers killed as "collateral damage." Perhaps ideologues so divorced from empathy are incapable of feeling even for themselves. Hence Timothy McVeigh's dead eyes and stoic stare into the camera as he lay on a gurney in the death chamber. Hence the unimaginable willingness of the men who sent those planes like fiery torpedoes into public buildings to see themselves, as well as their passengers, as merely incidental cargo in the service of some heinous greater good.

As the ground smokes and the people seethe, it is tempting to feel something of what those men did, to see human beings as a faceless bloc, a wholesale locus for anger and revenge. In the line to give blood at the Red Cross, a man railed against the Palestinians because he'd seen television

footage of men, women and children dancing for joy at the thousands of American dead. But that footage shows other people passing behind the gaudy celebrants, people unacknowledged by the outraged and the vengeful, people who look away, who do not join in. The Islamic Cultural Center a block away from here has a police officer standing guard; in the middle of the night the roar of a man's voice shatters the street nearby, crying, "Every sand n----r must die!" Crazy, perhaps, but with a crater of tumbled steel where two of the world's most iconographic buildings once stood, the people muttering conspiracies to themselves on the street have overnight come to seem like seers.

Amazing, isn't it, the sort of plotting and scheming and careful planning that the blazing belief in violence to underscore demagoguery can produce? Amazing, isn't it, that without any plotting or planning at all the notion that we are essentially alike leads human beings to rise up and, even stumbling about in the dark of horror, do what is necessary. Blood donations, bags of sandwiches, secondhand clothes, e-mail messages, casseroles, prayers, embraces. Evil requires careful machinations. Good does not. The end of the world came with both whimpers and bangs and all manner of sounds in between. When it was done, what hung over it all, greater than the smoke or the shock, was the sense of what most people are really made of, the emotional alchemy that enables us, from time to time, to love our neighbors as ourselves. To see ourselves in them all: the executives, the waiters, the lawyers, the police officers, the father, the mother, the 2-year-old girl off on an adventure, sitting safe between them, taking wing. ▮

"City of Ghosts" [EXCERPT]

by Tom Robbins and Jennifer Gonnerman, THE VILLAGE VOICE,
September 19–25, 2001

. . . Great tragedies leave behind legions of ghosts. They are the ghosts of those who perished, who would otherwise walk the streets, ride the subways and buses, dine in restaurants, toil at their jobs, laugh aloud in movie theaters, hold their children, make love to their partners. There one minute, they are suddenly disappeared, leaving only echoes, photographs, and intangible, ever-fading memories. . . .

How many died? The numbers, made purposefully vague by authorities fearful for public morale, are a moving target. On Monday, the estimate of those missing or dead stood at 5623. Gathered together, the victims would overflow the bleachers in Yankee Stadium.

But if the horrifying numbers are still imprecise, the ghosts have already assembled. They are there in the hundreds of posters created by distraught family members and friends, taped to trees, telephone booths, mailboxes, bus shelters, and vans. More than 1000 have been attached to the plywood "Wall of Prayer" at the entrance to Bellevue Hospital, just south of the grim East 30th Street offices of the city's medical examiner, where refrigerated trucks hold corpses and body parts. An astonishing number of the posters are computer-generated snapshots: pictures from weddings, from vacation cruises, from barbecues. Some are of businessmen and women posing proudly in front of the tall buildings that have become their likely tomb. Some, of parents with their children, read "Hurry Home Daddy."

The names are a New York symphony: Foti, Costello, Puckett, Barbella, Luparello, Morris, Faragher, Zinzi, Smith, Kumar, Ramos, Supinski, Bergstein, Barnes, Cho, Callahan, DeSantis, Wong, Dedvukaj, Villanueva, Cahill, Traina, Zeng. Even Rockefeller.

Likewise, the colors of the faces range from pale to dark, with every shade in between. Did the attackers imagine their victims? Did they picture the heathens they sought to punish as one class, one race, one color? If so, they failed miserably. The roster of the dead and the missing is inexorably democratic: There are investment bankers, secretaries, electricians, janitors, cops, firemen, photographers, delivery workers, bond brokers, cooks, waiters, dishwashers, lawyers, painters, and accountants. . . . ∎

ED BRADLEY | *Correspondent, CBS News:*

IN THOSE FIRST DAYS AFTER THE ATTACK on the World Trade Center, people from all over the city and the country descended upon Manhattan. They had given up their former lives or altered their days and nights to spend time at Ground Zero. They weren't there to gape and gawk. They were there to help.

Margie Edwards, the vice president of an investment bank in New Jersey, left her job every day and traveled to Pier 40, which was a volunteer hub along Manhattan's West Side Highway. There she organized the distribution of everything from snacks and water to work boots and gloves. She managed to get more than 100 companies to donate about $1 million in food and clothing.

Mike Orsa, originally from Brooklyn, drove a flatbed truck from North Carolina to New York and somehow found Edwards and her crew. Every night, he drove their supplies from Pier 40 to Ground Zero. "When my kids get older and study this in history," he said, "they will know that I was there and can say, 'My dad helped.' "

Sam Carle, a caterer in New York, used his experience as a mountain rescuer in the Colorado Rockies to crawl through the rubble looking for signs of life. He called his boss to tell her he'd be busy for a while.

Rusty Fleming and a band of recovering drug addicts and alcoholics drove up from Dallas. They had collected 30,000 pounds of meat, 12 cords of wood, and 2 smokers. They didn't know the Bronx from the Battery, but they stumbled across some Red Cross officials, who were trying to figure out how they were going to feed 2,000 people. "Sir, I think we can help you," said one of the Texans. Soon, the smell of BBQ shared the air with the burning rubble from Ground Zero.

And then there were the cops, the Highway Patrol under the command of Captain Kevin Hickey. They volunteered for one of the most wrenching jobs at Ground Zero: Whenever someone in uniform—a cop, a fireman, an emergency worker—was pulled from the wreckage, they saluted the body (or body part) and provided a ceremonial motorcycle escort to the city morgue for identification. One cop told me that it was the hardest thing he had ever done but it gave him a sense of satisfaction to provide a final moment of dignity.

These are just a few of the thousands of volunteers who were drawn by an overwhelming urge to help. I have always been impressed by that spirit in the American character that makes us reach out to others in a time of crisis. But I had never witnessed a reaction that was so visceral, so personal. All of these people seemed to be helping themselves, in addition to helping others.

"Not Just Another September Saturday" [EXCERPT]

by Manny Fernandez, Darragh Johnson, and Neely Tucker,
THE WASHINGTON POST, September 16, 2001

There are 58 steps leading up to the Lincoln Memorial, and each one served a different purpose yesterday. Down near the 20th, the young newlyweds posed for photos—the groom wearing his crisp green National Guard uniform, the bride a regal white wedding gown that dusted the marble and granite steps. They kissed to applause as people pretended, at least for a moment, not to hear sirens wailing in the distance.

Up near the 55th, a naval officer held his head in his hands and fought back tears as his family sat silent. There were many places for him to sit in Washington in the afternoon. But few offered the solace of this high perch—the Washington Monument in the distance, and behind them the sixteenth president's chiseled words calling for new dedication to the survival of free government. "It just kind of strikes home," the officer said.

Talk yesterday was of moving forward while looking back, a journey that brought some to tears and took others in search of normalcy to fairs and soccer games. Whether it was the 100 runners at the Compassion Dash 5K in Georgetown, or the few educators attending the student achievement conference at George Washington University, or even the church members of St. Thomas Episcopal in McLean, Va., who continued their annual yard sale—snippets of life resumed. Weddings went forward, and parents held new babies. Fathers took sons to T-ball practice in the District's Chevy Chase Park as thousands gathered for a merry olde time at the Maryland Renaissance Festival in Anne Arundel County, where Italianate troubadours and ladies in waiting adorned their costumes with red, white, and blue armbands and ribbons. "Life will never be the same, but everyone wants things to be familiar," said a decked-out Bruce Arnette, who traveled from Richmond to attend the festival, where a dollar from the admission price was designated to the Pentagon Survivors Fund.

But, everywhere, there was unease.

In a region where the national government is the biggest employer—where the national defense is both policy and an imposing military complex on the Potomac River—the attack struck home. If the target was the symbol of American military might, it was also where neighbors worked. . . .

For most of the week, the monuments that in many ways define Washington

were off-limits, fenced off and darkened. Even when they were briefly open, the threat of a sudden closing was there: U.S. Park Police officers, dressed in combat fatigues, altered the serenity of the Lincoln Memorial. On a moment's notice Thursday afternoon, officers on motorcycles, on horseback, and on foot evacuated visitors, draped police tape at the end of the Reflecting Pool, and sealed the area.

Yesterday morning, Park Police reevaluated the closing of the monuments, a move that "was precautionary to begin with," said Sergeant Rob MacLean, a Park Police spokesman. "The fact that security was relaxed around the White House factored into the decision that it was safe to open back up."

...On the steps of the Lincoln Memorial, the paths that often separate the classes, the races and the generations merged as one. Young, old, and in between sat together and talked quietly about the tragedy, some crying softly.

The steps offered people the rare chance of being alone while sitting together; it was a gift of solidarity and privacy, all at once.

Michael McCune and his wife, Dianne, both of Alexandria (Va.), had sat on these steps before and looked out on the capital skyline, the Washington Monument towering over the horizon like a thin marble steeple.

McCune is a Vietnam veteran and former navy pilot, and he said he realized how much he had taken the sight for granted. "We've been here probably a dozen times," said McCune, fifty-four. "We're seeing it with different eyes now." Here was Washington. Here, in the end, was America herself: Now more than ever, there was reason to sit and rest and cherish the view. ∎

STEVE KROFT | *Correspondent, CBS News:*

"IT IS JUST INCREDIBLE THAT 66 PEOPLE could be missing . . . and nothing. Nothing. Just gone." The look on Jimmy Dunne's face was one of disbelief, as if he was still trying to comprehend the inconceivable.

Dunne is the managing partner of Sandler O'Neil, a small investment-banking firm that had its offices on the 104th floor of Tower Two of the World Trade Center, but it had friends and customers all across the United States. Of the 83 people who reported for work on September 11, only 17 made it out of Tower Two alive, and they left the minute the first plane hit Tower One. The friends and co-workers who hesitated to call their families and tell them they were all right—"that the plane had hit the other building"—were not all right.

A few days after the attack, CBS News was allowed inside the small midtown office where the survivors of Sandler O'Neil had come to regroup. I recognized the look on their faces; I had seen it on soldiers emerging from battle, on refugees and survivors of natural disasters. Emotionally numb, physically drained, self-medicated with adrenaline, unable to completely grasp the enormity of events, yet focused on what had to be done. They were manning the phones, calling hospitals, sending out search parties for missing colleagues, consoling the families of friends who were dead or missing, and trying to reassemble the pieces of their lives.

The only alternative was to collapse in a heap or take to their beds. Work deadened the pain, made them relevant, and alive. They were trying to keep the enterprise going, keep the company afloat, for themselves, and for the wives, husbands, and children of Sandler O'Neil.

Entire departments had been wiped out: traders, number crunchers, researchers, clerks, rainmakers, partners. They made their money with their brains and personal relationships. Now that intellectual and personal capital was gone, along with the computers and the phone system, and every single piece of paper in the files.

Four days after the tragedy they had already moved into temporary quarters donated by Bank of America. Their competitors in the cutthroat world of Wall Street finance were offering equipment, people, and services—whatever Sandler O'Neil needed to stay in business. A group of programmers and software specialists who worked for a college roommate of Jimmy Dunne drove all night from Chicago and worked around the clock to get most of the communication systems up and running before the markets reopened. It was important. Not just for the country, but to show the people who had attacked their "little firm" and "killed their friends" that they were still there.

Before the opening bell of the New York Stock Exchange sounded the following Monday, a Sandler O'Neil manager named Terry Maltese looked out on a makeshift trading floor and rallied the troops. "Last Tuesday our friends were standing at their desks waiting for the market to open so they could make their trades. The market never opened. Our friends are gone, but they are watching us and we are not going to disappoint them. We are going to make those trades. People want to do business. Everyone wants to help us. And not doing it is not an option."

There were no tears. Tears were left for private moments and funerals. Across the front of the office on spreadsheets normally used to report sales and earnings were long lists of funerals and memorial services, two and three a day, well into the month of October.

Tom O'Neil, a surviving partner and founder of the firm, said, "I don't think we appreciated the depth of our enemies' hatred. But I think they have very much underestimated us."

In the days following the terrorist attacks on the World Trade Center, regular television programming was curtailed and replaced by 24-hour news coverage. But on Monday, September 17, 2001, David Letterman, the late-night talk-show host who broadcasts from New York City, was back on air. That night, Letterman spoke with Dan Rather of CBS News, who had anchored nearly 60 hours of four continuous days of news coverage. In a highly emotional interview, Rather spoke of the bravery of the firemen at Ground Zero and talked about the world being a new place and the American people facing a new kind of war in the aftermath of September 11.

PORTRAITS OF GRIEF

THE VICTIMS

Charming the Snake and the Husband; Making Fire Drills Count

Lydia Figueroa of Brooklyn and her granddaughter, also named Lydia, 3, added their names to the signatures, tributes and messages on a wall at the ground zero viewing platform on Friday. Recovery operations at the site officially melted last week.

PORTRAITS OF GRIEF

On September 15, 2001, The New York Times *started its "Portraits of Grief" page, which contained twelve to fifteen personal write-ups per day that honored the victims of September 11. For many readers of the* Times*, it was the first page they turned to in the morning. During a frightening period in history, the "Portraits of Grief" provided an opportunity for people to grieve and mourn for those who were lost.*

BILL GEIST | *Correspondent, CBS News:*

RIDGEWOOD, NEW JERSEY, is a small community of old homes, old trees, old values. It's where I live. From here you can get a spectacular view of New York's skyline, seventeen miles away.

It's a convenient commute to New York's downtown financial district, and early every morning my drowsy friends and neighbors grab coffee and bagels by the old, tiled-roof station and board trains for Wall Street, racing back home in the evening for family dinners, school plays, and soccer games.

On a sunny Tuesday in September, many did not come home. Twelve Ridgewood residents and many more from adjacent neighborhoods in towns that border ours were missing in the World Trade Center wreckage. Dozens more local families lost loved ones. Hundreds more narrowly escaped with their lives. Our town, our world, was shocked and transformed.

When you see little knots of people and parked cars in our town, it's always for a happy occasion—a backyard barbecue or a child's birthday party—but those clusters turned to somber gatherings of friends and neighbors who brought food and solace to the suffering, trying to shoulder some of the grief.

Flags flew at half-mast, and they flew everywhere. "The View," as it's known, the scenic vista of Manhattan that's normally a place of beauty and romance, became a memorial, its rock wall bedecked with flowers, candles, flags, and messages.

In our little park at the center of town, where teenagers skateboard and children line up in December to visit Santa, candlelight vigils were held. Our local newspaper, which normally carries front-page headlines about delightfully innocuous non-events, now reported hard news on the local dead. Our places of worship kept their doors open at all hours, and people came to pray and cry quietly.

Everyone in town desperately wanted to do something, anything, to help. At dawn each day, a team of local firefighters went to the World Trade Center site to aid in the recovery efforts. Our hospital geared up to care for an influx of injured, but sadly there weren't any. At the library an emergency-counseling center was set up, staffed with volunteer counselors. There were long lines at the local blood bank. Children sold lemonade from curbside card tables for the cause.

The local Red Cross office was abuzz. Volunteers sorted a small mountain of donated items and loaded them on supply trucks bound for rescue workers in the city. Others answered phones, as thousands of calls came in offering money, goods, and manual labor. People signed up for disaster relief lessons held in classrooms that were standing-room-only.

"People feel such an intense overwhelming need to do something," said Susan, who was working in the Red Cross office, answering one call after another. "They want to be there. They want to try and help find somebody. They want to pull away the concrete and glass and they don't ask, 'Is it risky?' "

"The worst in the human experience has brought out the most glorious in the human spirit," said Reverend Tom Marsden, pastor of a local church. "In their numbness and pain, people have reached out."

On the first weekend after the tragedy, the full schedule of football and soccer games and such were all canceled, along with the big street fair, the village employees' picnic, and an outdoor concert. Instead there were more candlelight vigils and prayer services. There were still commuter cars parked at the train station that Tuesday morning that had not been picked up.

The Saturday before September 11, I had a beer at an afternoon porch party with my friend Jon Vandevender. Jon went to work that Tuesday on his usual early train headed for his office on the ninety-second floor of the North Tower (Tower 1) of the World Trade Center. During the attacks, he talked to his wife, Annie, and their son, Jonny, on the phone a few times. Annie's sister called me to ask if I knew someone to call who might know a back way out for Jon. Minutes later, the building collapsed.

Friends and neighbors came by their house in droves to do what they could to comfort Annie, and their three children, Jonny, fourteen, Janey, nine, and Molly, five, as well as Jon's mother and brother. Janey tried for days to reach her father on his cell phone, but Annie told her children that their father was probably not coming home.

Julie Sztjenberg called me and my wife to say her mother, Gina, had been working in the World Trade Center and was gone. They had been our next-door neighbors. My kids grew up with theirs. Gina rode to work every morning with her husband, Mike, who also worked in the financial district. The two were inseparable, having grown up together in Poland, and when their families moved to New York they found each other, married, and made a life together.

Jon's body was found, one of the few. It is a measure of the magnitude of this tragedy that Annie said she considered herself "lucky." His memorial service was the first in a long fall season of them in our community, and began in a most unconventional fashion with the playing of Bruce Springsteen's "Thunder Road," Jon's favorite song. In the days ahead there would be lots of such unorthodox funeral music wafting from church windows. All of the victims died young.

They speak of the untold number of lives touched in this overwhelming catastrophe that killed thousands. And just look. At Jon's service a thousand people—from the local pizza man, to the golf pro, to kids Jon coached, to his neighbors, and college friends—packed the church. Hundreds more stood outside and watched the service on a screen set up in the parking lot.

Gina and Mike were not particularly active in the community, yet about a thousand people came for her service, as surprised attendants at the temple set up folding chairs as fast as they could.

Allison Sharkey is a friend of ours, a young woman who recently married and became pregnant. She was also working in the World Trade Center that day. She and a group of her colleagues found a back stairwell somehow and escaped. She had a baby boy in the spring and gave him the middle name of a co-worker who did not make it out alive.

To this tranquil town that has always provided us refuge from the pressure, pandemonium, and problems of the outside world, monstrous evil came halfway round the world to set upon New York and reach with deadly tentacles through the tunnel and up the railway tracks. Ridgewood, and America, which had never been the target of foreign attacks, would never be the same.

It left untold misery among the survivors, who asked how this could happen and why. Parishioners packed our local churches and synagogues seeking answers to some very tough questions.

When Annie told Molly that God had pulled her father up to heaven from this massive disaster, five-year-old Molly asked, "Does God have enough hands?"

Permissions Acknowledgments